1 MONTH OF
FREE
READING

at
www.ForgottenBooks.com

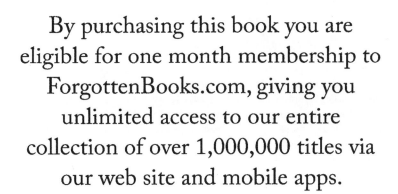

By purchasing this book you are eligible for one month membership to ForgottenBooks.com, giving you unlimited access to our entire collection of over 1,000,000 titles via our web site and mobile apps.

To claim your free month visit:

www.forgottenbooks.com/free892712

ISBN 978-0-266-80894-7

PIBN 10892712

UNITED STATES STORE CARDS

A List of Merchants' Advertising Checks, Restaurant
Checks, and Kindred Pieces Issued from 1789 up
to Recent Years, Including Many of the Tokens
Which Passed as Money and Known as
Hard Times Tokens

BY
EDGAR H. ADAMS

NEW YORK, 1920

Introduction

In preparing this list of store cards, &c., the compiler has been guided by no particular rule, but has listed together with regular advertising cards other items which have for many years been popular with collectors of series of this kind. The collection of store cards and kindred objects was much more in favor many years ago, with such well-known and indefatigable collectors as J. N. T. Levick, Benjamin Betts, Elliott Woodward, Charles Morris, Dr. B. P. Wright and others. The collection of Mr. Levick, which was sold in 1884, was at that time by far the most complete, and today the catalogue of that sale is invaluable as a guide to the collectors. Mr. Betts' collection was also a very noteworthy one, and was particularly remarkable for the series of New York store cards, although it also contained many rare and desirable pieces belonging to other localities. Mr. Betts' collection was sold in 1908, and the catalogue furnishes, with its interesting historical notes and plates, another very necessary guide to collectors. Mr. Woodward's collection was disposed of in 1884 and contained a very complete series. The collection of Dr. Wright has been sold at various intervals, and ranks with the Levick collection for completeness. Dr. Wright probably has given the subject more attention than any one else, and wrote a list of the pieces in his collection, which was published in the Numismatist in 1900 and 1901. A very interesting and complete list of the store cards of New York was published in The Coin Collectors' Journal in 1885, 1886 and 1887. This same list was reprinted by the New York Numismatic Club in 1913. In 1907 F. G. Duffield of Baltimore, prepared a very comprehensive list of store cards and kindred items of Maryland for the Numismatist. There are other sales of store cards which are important, such as that held by Geo. A. Leavitt & Co., of New York in 1890, "the property of a well-known Brooklyn collector.'' This contained a very complete series, other than those of New York, among which were a number of the great rarities, such as the Walton cards of New Orleans, Huckel, Burrows & Jennings of St. Louis, and Loomis of Cleveland, Ohio.

There are quite a number of items in the present list which cannot be called store cards, and yet we think the predilection of collectors for tiem entitles them to be added. We refer particularly to the member checks of the various jockey clubs, the drayage checks, and also the restaurant checks. The latter form an extensive series, especially those of New York City, and recall many old-time establishments long since passed away and bring to mind the period of New York's history when money values were reckoned in shillings and pence.

It is recognized that the extensive nature of the subject treated entails many omissions. Tiese will be rectified from time to time in future editions, when illustration will be furnished together with such information as may come to hand. The compiler will be very grateful to have omissions brought to his attention, and thanks readers in advance for any courtesy tiat may be extended.

The small tradesmen's tokens issued during the civil war from 1861 to 1864, inclusive, are not included in this list, but will be made the subject of another list, which will be published later.

In getting this list together a great deal of help has been given by various persons who are interested in the subject and it is desired to especially thank Messrs. Howland Wood, David Proskey, Wayte Raymond, Henry Chapman and F. C. C. Boyd for their generous assistance and the American Numismatic Society for the opportunity accorded to closely examine its fine store card collection.

ALABAMA.

MOBILE.

1   HUNT, PYNCHON & JACKSON. Hardware and Cutlery. Anvil etc. Brass. Excessively rare.

2   MOBILE JOCKEY CLUB 1853. Member's medal. Horse. ℞ NOT TRANSFERABLE. Brass.

3   Same. Copper.

4   Same. Silver.

5   Same. White metal.

6   Same. Copper-nickel.

7   Same obverse. ℞ Cupid and dolphin. Copper.

8   Same. Brass.

9   Same. White metal.

10   Same. Silver.

11   Same. Copper-nickel.

12   Same obverse. ℞ Witch on broom. Copper.

13   Same. Brass.

14   Same. White metal.

15   Same. Silver.

16   Same. Copper-nickel.

17   Same obverse. ℞ Daniel Webster. Copper.

18   Same. Brass.

19   Same. White metal.

20   Same. Silver.

21   Same. Copper-nickel.

22   Same obverse. ℞ Edwin Forrest. Copper.

23   Same. Brass.

24   Same. White metal.

25   Same. Silver.

26   Same. Copper-nickel.

NOTE.—The preceding reverses are also minted with the NOT TRANS-FERABLE reverse, but as they bear no name they are omitted .

MONTGOMERY.

27   STICKNEY & WILSON. Dry goods, etc. Brass. Reeded edge. Very rare.

SELMA.

28   SYLVESTER & CO. Merchant Tailors. Brass. Plain edge.

29   Same obverse. ℞ New York Crystal Palace. A mule. Copper. Very rare.

CALIFORNIA.

SACRAMENTO.

1   J. L. POLHEMUS DRUGGIST 190 J. ST. COR 7th.   Counterstamp on New Granada dollar 1839.

2   Same on U. S. Dollar of 1843.

SAN FRANCISCO.

3   BERENHART, JACOBY & CO. General Merchants.   ℞ Ship.   Brass. 26m.

4   FRANK, W. & CO. Importers. Brass. 27m.

5   HYMAN, N. J. Watches and Jewelry. Copper. 31m.

6   JOSEPH BROS., Watchmakers, etc. Brass. Reeded edge. 30m.

7   KELLEY, WM., 186 Kearney St. Head of Liberty to l.   ℞ Eagle. Trial piece in lead. Have seen only one specimen.

8   MAUDIT. CERCLE DE SAN FRANCISCO ½ DOLLAR. White metal. 27m. Very rare.

9   THURNAUER & ZINN. Large C in circle. ℞ Liberty head. Brass. 27m.

10   THURNAUER & ZINN. Importers of Baskets, Toys and Fancy Goods. (TANCY). ℞ Liberty head. Brass. 27m.

11   Similar to preceding but FANCY. Brass. 22m.

12   WEIL & LEVI. Importers of Fancy Goods. Brass. 27½m. Only one known.

CONNECTICUT.

BRIDGEPORT.

1   PLATT, O. S. 99 Cannon St., Pattern Making, etc. Valve in center. Copper, cast. Very rare.

BRISTOL.

2   BOTSFORD, S. N. & H. C. Medical Electrical Apparatus.   ℞ Eagle. Brass.

3   Similar. ℞ THADDEUS SMITH, AGENT FOR APPARATUS. Brass.

COLCHESTER.

4   HAYWARD. N. ℞ Blank. White metal. 36m. (Bangs sale, May 1, 1863).

FAIR HAVEN.

5   CHAMBERLAIN, WOODRUFF & SCRANTON. ℞ HOTCHKISS, HALL. & PLATTS LONG BRICK STORE. Brass.

HARTFORD.

6 ROBINSON, ALFRED, S. BANKER, BROKER, NOTARY PUBLIC, ETC. ℞ Representation of the store of Day, Griswold & Co., 54 Asylum St. Copper. 28m. Only one specimen known. J. Coolidge Hills Collection in Wadsworth Athenaeum, Hartford.

7 ROBINSON, ALFRED S. BANKER, NUMISMATIST, NOTARY PUBLIC, ETC. ℞ Copy of Higley threepence, deer obverse. Silver. 28m.

8 Same. Copper.

— 9 Same. Brass.

10 Same. White metal.

11 Same. Copper-nickel.

12 ROGERS, SMITH & CO. "Extra Plate on White Metal." ℞ Blank. White metal. 26m.

13 ROGERS, SMITH & CO. Number in centre. ℞ Blank. White metal. 32m.

NEW HAVEN.

14 BASSETT & CO. J. E. Hardware. ℞ Advertising card. Copper.

15 Same obverse. ℞ Skate with scroll below. Copper.

16 BETTS, C. W. NUMISMATIST. Copper. Rude impression.

17 Same. Lead.

18 Similar. COINS, MEDALS etc. Copper. Rude impression.

19 Same. Head.

20 CELLULOID STARCH CO. "A Great Invention Free." Mullet after CO. Brass.

_ 21 Similar. Star after CO. Brass.

22 Similar. No period after CO. ℞ "A Great Invention, Present." Large period close to N. Brass.

—.. 23 Similar. Small period distant from N. Brass.

24 Similar. Reverse inscription in eight straight lines. Brass.

25 DAVENPORT. Combs, Perfumery, etc. Copper.

— 26 FOBES & BARLOW, SASH & BLIND MFGS. Copper.

27 WATERBURY HOUSE, 42 CHURCH ST. N. H. ℞ 4, two dogs below running to l. Ornamental border. Brass. 20m. Rare.

WATERBURY.

— 28 BENEDICT & BURNHAM. Mfgs. of Gilt Buttons, etc. ℞ Eagle. Low 109. Brass.

29 BROWN & BROS. Brass Works. Various numbers on reverse. Brass. 20m.

30 HAYDEN, F. Retrograde letters. Struck over U. S. Cent. Very rare.

31 HOLMES, BOOTH & HAYDEN. ℞ Blank. Nickel silver.

32 HOLMES, BOOTH & HAYDEN. Mfgs. of Lamp Goods. Copper, nickel. 20m.

33 SCOVILL, J. M. L. & W. H. Mfgs. of Naval Military Crests, Fine Plain. Gilt & Plated and all kinds of Fancy Buttons. ℞ View of factory buildings. White metal. 37m. Excessively rare.

34 SCOVILL, J. M. L. & W. H. Mfgs. of Sheet Brass, etc. ℞ Phoenix. Low
      130. Copper. Scarce.
35 SCOVILL. J. M. L. & W. H. Brass. Scarce.
36 WATERBURY BRASS CO. Brass token used in the works with various
      numbers on reverse. 23m.
37 Similar. WATERBURY, CONN. on reverse. 19m.

DELAWARE.

1   RANDEL, J. Jr. (1825 in wreath) C. & D. Canal. ℞ Blank. Copper.
2   Similar. Target centre. Copper.

GEORGIA.

AUGUSTA.

1   GILBERT, I. Saddlery Warehouse. Copper. Very rare.
2   Same. Brass. Extremely rare.
3   MORRISON, J. & D. Grocers. Copper. Excessively rare.

SAVANNAH.

4   ELDORADO SALOON. 10 in center. German silver. 28m.
5   HAYWOODS SALOON. 10 in center. Nickel. 28m.
6   Similar. 25 in center. Nickel. 27m.
7   HAUSMAN, W. H. Blue Store, Clothing Warehouse. Brass. 22m.

ILLINOIS.

BELVIDERE.

1   PLANE, JOHN & CO. 1856. Hardware & Stoves. Anvil. ℞ Stove.
      Brass.
2   Same. Copper.
3   PLANE & JENNISON, Hardware, etc. Similar type to preceding. Brass.

CHICAGO.

4   BAKER & MOODY, HATTERS. Eagle. ℞ Hat. Copper. Plain
      edge.
5   Same. Brass.
6   Same. Brass, thin planchet.
7   Same. Brass. Milled edge, Thick planchet.
8   BURBANK & SHAW. 1845. Dry Goods, etc. Copper.
9   CHILDS & CO. 1858. Eagle. ℞ View of Chicago Court House. Cop-
      per. Rare.
10 Similar without eagle. ℞ Same as preceding. Brass. Rare.

11 CHILDS. Die Sinker and Engraver. 1860. 117½ Randolph St. Liberty seated. Brass. 20m.

12 HAMILTON & WHITE. 1845. Dry Goods and Produce. Prairie schooner to r. Copper.

13 HANNAH & HOAG, 222, 224 Clark St., German silver. 25m.

14 HOLDEN, C. N. & CO. Dry Goods & Groceries. Brass. Milled edge.

15 Same. Copper. Plain edge.

16 Same. Brass, silvered.

17 Obverse of preceding muled with obverse of token of Francisco & Whitman, Nashville, Tenn. Copper, silvered. Plain edge.

18 JENSCH, F. A. BELL FOUNDER. Copper.

19 Same. Brass.

20 Same. White metal.

21 J. H. H.—COURT HOUSE above view of structure. Below 1858— CHICAGO. ℞ J. H. H. 272 Incuse. Brass. 26m.

22 PEACOCK, C. D. Jeweler. Peacock with head to r. 1837 below (not contemporary with date). Copper.

23 Same. Silver.

24 Similar. Peacock with head to l. Copper.

25 PEARSON & DANA. BOOTS & SHOES. Copper.

26 Same. Brass.

27 SHAW, J. B. BOOKSELLER. Badly double struck on a silver counterfeit of a gold dollar. In the cabinet of the American Numismatic Society, probably unique.

28 SCHUTTLER, PETER. WAGON MANUFACTURER, 45 West Munroe St. Chicago. View of the Pioneer Wagonworks. Brass.

29 Same. Brass, silvered.

30 Same. White metal.

31 Same. Name of agent at Austin, Texas. Brass.

32 Same. Name of agent at Dallas, Texas. Brass.

33 Same. Name of agent at Kansas City, Mo. Brass.

34 Same. Name of agent at Iowa City, Ia. Brass.

35 Same. Name of agent at San Francisco, Cal. Brass.

36 Same. Name of agent at Sherman, Texas. Brass.

37 Same. Name of agent at Denver, Col. Brass.

38 Same. Name of agent at Portland, Ore. Brass.

39 Same. Name of agent at Cheyenne, Wyo. Brass.

40 STUMPS, PETER. Boot & Shoe maker, 188 State St. ℞ Fireman's Hat. Brass. 22m.

41 WILLOUGHBY, HILL & CO. Boston Square Dealing Clothing Store.

INDIANA.

CRAWFORDSVILLE.

1   HILDEBRAND & CO. C. S.   Watch makers.   ℞ Murdock, Cincinnati, O. Brass.

INDIANAPOLIS.

2   Parry Mfg. Co.   Mfgs. of Buggies, etc.   Copper.

IOWA.

McGREGER.

1   KOHN, A. & CO.   Clothing.   ℞ Carpenters Hall.   White metal.

WINTERSET.

2   PUTZEE'S CLOTHING.   ℞ Independence Hall.   White metal.

KENTUCKY.

LOUISVILLE.

1   BROWN, CURTISS & VANCE.   Dry Goods.   Eagle.   447 Market St. Brass.
2   Same obverse.   ℞ Reverse of Taylor & Raymond card.   Copper.   A mule.
3   Same obverse.   ℞ C. W. Jackson.   Broad & Lombard Sts.   Coal Dealers.   Copper.
4   Same obverse.   ℞ Blank.   Copper.
5   COOK & SLOSS, Jewelers.   ℞ Louisville Industrial Exposition building.   Brass.   26m.
6   Same obverse.   ℞ Locomotive, PROGRESS above.   Brass.
7   DUNCAN, SANDFORD.   Silks, etc.   Eagle.   Copper.   Plain edge.
8   Same.   Silvered.
9   Same.   Brass.   Milled edge.
10   Same.   Brass.   Plain edge.
11   Same obverse.   ℞ Three umbrellas, etc., reverse design of Richardson card of Philadelphia.   Brass.
12   Same obverse.   ℞ Public Square, Nashville, Tenn.   Hat.   Copper. Mule. Rare.
13   Same.   White metal.
14   HIRSCHBUHL, J. J.   Incuse.   German silver.   22m.
15   HOWE MACHINE CO.   Bust of Elias Howe.   ℞ Locomotive.   Brass.
16   HOWE MACHINE CO.   "Buy a Howe machine for cash etc."   ℞ Exposition building.   Brass.
17   Same obverse.   ℞ Locomotive.   Brass.
18   Mule.   Exposition building.   ℞ Locomotive.   Brass.

19 J. J. F.—ST. CHARLES. ℞ LOUISVILLE, KY. Silver. 13½ m.
   Very rare.
20 KIRTLAND, F. S. Clothing ℞ Exposition building. Brass.
21 Same obverse. ℞ Locomotive.
22 LURIA, M. H. Watches & Jewelry. Eagle. Silver. Excessively rare.
23 Same. Copper. Excessively rare.
24 MILLER, H. & CO. Engravers, etc. Silver. 33m.
25 Same. Copper.
26 Same. White metal.
27 PREUSER & WELLENVOSS. Hatters. ℞ Exposition building. Brass.
28 Same obverse. ℞ Locomotive. Brass.
29 PREISSLER, H. Nickel. 20m.
30 QUEST, J. W. Boots & Shoes. ℞ Exposition building. Brass.
31 Same obverse. ℞ Locomotive.
32 TAYLOR & RAYMOND. Gentleman's Furnishing Store. Eagle.
   Brass. Rare. (This reverse was used for a number of mules).
33 THOMAS, H. E. & CO. Hardware Store. Reverse is a copy of hardware implements as on obverse of Canadian token, of T. S. Brown
   & Co. White metal. Excessively rare.
34 WHALEY, SHERMAN P., Clothing. Brass. Rare.
35 WOLF, GEORGE, Jeweler. ℞ View of bridge. White metal.

JEFFERSON COUNTY.

36 SUIT, S. T., 1750. Salt River Bourbon. Copper. Plain edge.
37 Same. Brass. Milled edge.
38 Same. Silvered before striking. Milled edge.
39 Same. White metal. Plain edge.
40 Same obverse. ℞ BALDWIN & CO. PATENT APRIL 18, 1858, all
   incuse. Brass. 28m. Rare.

HENDERSON.

41 JOHNSON & BROS. White metal. 19m.

LAWRENCE.

42 R. L. FRAZER, JEWELER, LAWRENCE, KT. cs. on 1853 quarter
   dollar. Rare.

LOUISIANA.

NEW ORLEANS.

1 ALBERT, J. J. HAT IMPORTER. Copper. 24m. Very rare.
2 ALBERT & TRICOU. HATS. Copper. 24m. Rare
3 Same German silver. Rare.
4-5-6 DAQUIN BROS. Bakers. GOOD FOR ONE LOAF OF BREAD. ℞
   BON POUR UN PAIN. Brass. Ten sided. 23m. Rare.

7   Similar. Differing dies. GOOD FOR on one line. Period after PAIN
     on reverse, stars smaller. Brass. 23m. Rare.

8   EDGAR, W. J. Clothing. Brass. 26m. Rare.

9   FOLGER, NATHAN C. 1837. Clothing, Hats, Shoes, etc. By Bale &
     Smith. Brass. 35m. Low 121. Excessively rare.

10   FOLGER N. C. CLOTHING, etc. 17 Old Levee. Eagle. Leaf orna-
     ments on reverse. TRUNKS. Copper. Reeded edge. BLANKETS,
     etc.

11   Same. Brass.

12   Same. Brass. Silvered.

13   Similar. CLOTHING, CAPS, BLANKETS. Silver. Extremely rare.

14   Same. Brass. Reeded edge.

15   Same. Copper. Reeded edge.

16   Similar obverse. Figure "7" even with "1." Star ornaments on re-
     verse. R Reverse of card of Taylor & Raymond, Louisville. A
     mule. Brass. Reeded edge.

17   Same. Copper. Reeded edge.

18   Similar. Second reverse, high "7." Brass. Plain edge.

19   Similar obverse. R Card of C. W. Jackson, Philadelphia. Copper. A
     mule.

     NOTE.—There are quite a number of die varieties of the Folger cards,
         with trifling differences.

20   FOLGER, N. C. Similar but eagle has drooping wings. Brass. Reeded
     edge.

21-22 FOLGER, N. C. & SON. CLOTHING. A swan. R Crescent. Brass,
     Reeded edge.

23   Same. Brass. Plain edge.

24   FOLGER & BLAKE, Clothing Store. Eagle. Similar to the one in
     silver. No. 13. Brass. Reeded edge. See Numismatist 1915. Page
     169.

25   GAINES, CHAS. C. HARDWARE, CUTLERY, etc. R Padlock. Silver.
     Plain edge. Excessively rare.

26   Same. Brass. Excessively rare.

27   GASQUET, PARISH & CO. 47 Chartres St. R Eagle. Brass. Very
     rare.

28   GOWANS, D. & CO. CONFECTIONERS. Copper. 22m.

29   Same. Copper, silvered.

30   HENDERSON & GAINES, Importers of China, Glass, etc. Brass. Plain
     edge. 33m. Very rare.

31   Same. White metal. Excessively rare.

32   HENDERSON, WALTON & CO. Importers of China, Glass, etc. Same.
     reverse as on preceding. Brass. 33m. Very rare.

33   JACOBS, E. DAGUERREOTYPES. Liberty head. R Eagle. Copper.
     Plain edge.

34   Same. Brass. Reeded edge.

35   Same. Brass. Plain edge.

36   Same. Copper, silvered.

37   Same. White metal. Rare.

38 LYONS, L. W. & CO. Clothings, Trunks, etc. View of their building. 2 dies. ℞ Eagle. Brass. 24m. Reeded edge.
39 Same. Copper. Plain edge.
40 Same. Nickel or German silver.. Plain edge. Rare.
41 MERLE, JOHN A. & CO. Bienville Street. ℞ Eagle. Brass. Reeded edge. Rare.
42 PITKIN, ROBERT, Clothing, Trunks, etc. View of building. Brass. Reeded edge. 24m.
43 PUECH, BEIN & CO. 1834. Importers of Hardware, Guns, Pistols, etc. Copper. 25m. Low 82. Excessively rare.
44 P. B. (Puech, Bein & Co.) script in circle of rings counterstamped on quarter section of Spanish 8 reales. ℞ NOUVELLE ORLEANS and eagle counterstamp. Silver. Very rare.
45 TATOUT BROTHERS, Importers of Fancy Goods, Brass. 23m. Octagonal. Plated center. Very rare.
46 THEODORE, 150 CHARTRES St. Copper.- 23m. Octagonal. Very rare.
47 Same. Brass. Very rare.
48 WALKER, J. HALL & WALTON 1834. Importers of Hardware and Ship Chandlery. Brass. 33m. Extremely rare. Low 85.
49 WALTON, WALKER & CO. 1836. The same firm as preceding. Similar wording. Brass. 33m. Extremely rare. Low 106.
50 WALTON & CO. Without date. The same firm as preceding under a still different name. Brass. 33m. Extremely rare.
51 YALE, C. Jr. & Co. Silk and Straw Goods. Brass. Rare.
52 Same. Copper. Rare.

MAINE.

BANGOR.

1 N. H. BRAGG & SON, BANGOR, ME. Stamped on 1845 cent.

BIDDEFORD.

2 McKENNEY, GUNSMITH, BIDDEFORD incused on 1848 Cent.

BRUNSWICK.

3 FIELD, W. R. 25. White metal.

FARMINGTON.

4 GREENWOOD & CO., CHESTER. EAR PROTECTORS, &c. Brass.

WATERFORD.

5 DR. SHATTUCK'S WATER CURE, WATERFORD, ME, incused on 1853 quarter dollar.
6 Same. Stamped on quarter dollar of 1854.

YORK.

7 QUEBE, F., YORK, ME. Undraped bust of Washington. White metal. Very thick planchet. Excessively rare.

MARYLAND.

ANNAPOLIS.

1 BAKER, W. R., Fruit-Packer . ℞ Female head. Brass. 25m. Duffield 3.

--

BALTIMORE.

2 ACCOMMODATION LINE. ℞ "Omnibus." Silver, or plated. 18m. D. 1.
3 ANCHOR HOTEL. "J. H. Benjes, Prop." &c. ℞ An anchor. Aluminum. 24m.
4 L. A. (ASBECK.) "Mystic." ℞ "5." Brass. 20m. D. 2.
5 "B. L." in monogram of script letters. figure "5" Brass. 20m. D. 4.
6 Same obverse. "25." Nickel. 20m. D. 5.
7 BALTIMORE TOKEN, The. Ship sailing. ℞ shield in circle of 13 stars. Brass. Thick planchet. 23m. D. 6.
8 Same as last, but small stars and thin planchet. D. 7.
9 B. U. P. Ry. Co. Transfer. ℞ Good Only at Transfer Station. Copper. 25m. D. 8.
10 BARNES, S. S., & Co., Oyster Planters and Packers. ℞ An oyster in circle of 16 stars. Brass. 21m. D. 9.
11 "33 & 35 E. Baltimore St." ℞ "Free Pool." An elephant in the centre. All incuse, Nickel. 25m. The card of Joseph Beard, Jr. D. 10.
12 BELT, WM., & CO., Leather Manufacturers. ℞ eagle. Brass. 29m. D. 11.
13 BIBB, (B. C.) Stove Co. ℞ inscription. Brass. 25m. D. 12.
14 Same. Copper. D. 12.
15 BLOCK (EDWARD) & CO. In centre "5." Reverse same as obverse. D. 13.
16 BROOKS, GEO. D. Canton Can Works. In the centre "100." ℞ 25 in wreath. Nickel. 20m. D. 15.
17 BUCK, G. W. ℞ "Good for One Drink." Silver. 16m. D. 16.
18 "C., J. W., & CO. 1 Gal." ℞ female head, 1875. Brass. 20m.
19 CALF HIDE ASSOC. OF BALTO. CITY. 10. "Incuse figures. ℞ "Class D. 180." Incuse. Brass. 25m. D. 17.
20 Same, but "5" in centre. Rev. "Class F 23." Brass. 25m.
21 CALVERTON CLUB. Rooster in centre. Rev. "5" in wreath. Copper. 20m. D. 18.
22 Same, but "10." Nickel. D. 19.
23 CARROLLTON CLOTHING HOUSE. ℞ Liberty head. 1876. Brass. 25m. D. 20.
24 CASINO No. 3. An eagle in centre. Rev. "25." in wreath. German silver. 20m. D. 21.
25 Same, but "10·" Copper. 20m.
26 CENTRAL RAILWAY CO. In the centre a large "C" in the planchet. "Good for One Child's Fare." Copper. 20m. D. 22.

27 CENTRAL PASS. R. R. CO. Within a circle "½," ℞ "Half Fare Ticket." Within circle "½." Brass. 20m. D. 23.

28 CHAPMAN, JOHN L. In centre "One Soda." Rev. eagle. Silver, or plated. 17m. D. 24.

29 Obverse and reverse similar, but 13 stars around eagle. Below "BALE" incused. Silver or plated. 17m. D. 25.

30 CHAPMAN, JOHN L. Below, "Baltimore." ℞ inscription. Silver. 17m. D. 26.

31 Same. Copper. D. 26.

32 CLARIDGE, G. D., & CO., Dealers in Dairy Products. ℞ Liberty head. 1875. Brass. 20m. D. 27.

33 Similar to last, but no period after "o" of "Co." Nor after "Products." or "Baltimore." A period after "D." ℞ same as last. Brass. 20m.

34 CLOUD HOUSE. below, "D. & R." In centre "5c·" Rev. plain. Brass 24m. D. 28.

35 COLE, H. H, Importer and Manufacturer of Clothing Costume Hall. Brass. 28m. D. 29.

36 Same. German silver. Very rare.

37 COLE, JAMES. Fells Point. ℞ ship. Copper. 23m. D. 30.

38 Same. Brass. D. 30.

39 CONCORDIA. In center "5." ℞ eagle, Copper. 22m· D. 31.

40 Same, but "10·" Brass.

41 Same, but "25·" Nickel. D. 32.

42 DORMAN'S STENCIL & STAMP WORKS, 19 German St. ℞ Liberty head. 1875. Brass. 20m. D. 33.

43 Same, but "19 German St." in larger letters. D. 34.

44 DORMAN, J. F. W., Man'f'r of Printing Presses 21 German St., Baltimore. (the word's "Printing Presses" on two scrolls. ℞ "Dorman's stencil and stamp works, Baltimore." In centre "25" in large figures. Brass. D. 35.

45 DORMAN, J. F. W., Manufacturer of Printing Presses. ℞ "5" in rays. Brass, silver plated. 20m. D. 36.

46 ELLIOTT, H. A., & BRO. in Centre, 1853. ℞ "One Soda" in wreath. Nickel. 20m. D. 37.

47 EVENING NEWS. In centre, "15," incused. ℞ plain. Copper. 24m. D. 38.

57 GEEKIE, CHAS. W. "5" in centre. ℞ "Ladies Blush." An anchor
and two decanters. White metal. D. 46.

58 Same. German silver.

59 Same, but "10" in centre. White metal.

60 KOLA PEPSIN, &c. ℞ "Good for One Glass Kola Pepsin," &c. Aluminum. Size 29m. D. 47.

61 GERMANIA MAENNERCHOR. ℞ figure "5." in wreath. Copper.
22m. D. 48.

62 Same, but "10." D. 49.

63 GOSMAN & CO. In centre a soda fountain. ℞ "10" in wreath. Nickel.
22m. D. 52.

64 GRANNISS & TAYLOR ℞. Omnibus and two horses. Brass. Oval.
16x23m. D. 53.

65 GUTH CHOCOLATE CO. ℞ eagle and inscription. Brass. 29m. D. 54.

66 GUTMAN, JOEL, & CO. ℞ "10" in rays. Nickel. 20m. D. 55.

– 67 HAMILL, CHAS. W., & CO., Silver Plated Ware. ℞ Baltimore Battle
Monument, "October, 1880." White metal and gilded. 28m. D. 56.

68 HARDY, COL., Crier. 1858. Brass. 24m. D. 57.

69 HERRING H., FAIRMOUNT. ℞ the date 1834 within circle of olive
leaves, White metal. 35m. (Low 173). D. 58. Extremely rare.

70 HOCHSCHILD, KOHN & CO. Maryland coat of arms. ℞ plain. Copper. 20m. D. 59.

71 HORN, H. J. & CO. Below, "Baltimore." In centre, "5." Rev. female head. Brass. D. 60.

72 HOUCK'S PANACEA, BALTIMORE Counterstamped on silver dollar
of 1795. D. 61.

73 Same. On half dollar of 1830. D. 62.

74 Same. On half dollar of 1833.

75 W. H. J. Rev. large figure "5." over circle of rays. Brass. D. 63.

76 BENJAMIN JURY. Below, "Baltimore." Within a wreath "Vaux
Hall." ℞ figure of Liberty. 1848. German silver. D. 64.

77 KANN'S BUSY CORNER. Bust of Admiral Dewey. 1899. Brass.
D. 65.

78 KEACH. BALTIMORE STREET. In centre, "One Soda." ℞ eagle.
D. 66. German silver.

79 KENNY, C. D., CO. Teas, Coffees, Sugars. Bust of Schley. Aluminum.
D. 67.

80 KENSETT. ℞ same as obverse. Brass. D. 68.

81 KEPLER'S, 5 NORTH ST. Balto. Aluminum. D. 69.

82 KEPLER'S, 113 Park Ave. Balto. Aluminum. D. 70.

83 KNIGHT. A., 99 BALTO. ST. ℞ "Mineral Water." German silver.
D. 71.

84 KNIGHT'S MINERAL SALOON, counterstamped on U. S. quarter dollar. D. 72.

85 Same, counterstamped on Spanish two-real piece. D. 73.

86 KUNKEL'S OPERA TROUPE. Counterstamped on Mexican two-reals
of 1744. D. 75.

87 MARWELL, W. G., 166 Baltimore St. Vulcanite. D. 79.

88 MASON, BAKER. Rev. sheaf of wheat. Brass. D. 80.

89 MECHANICS HALL, 152 FAYETTE ST. ℞ "Good for 5 Cents." Brass Octagonal. D. 83.

90 MITCHELL, J. PEOPLES LINE. ℞ an omnibus, drawn by two horses. Brass. Oval. D. 84.

91 MOMENTHY, B., FAYETTE HALL, BALTIMORE. ℞ figure "5" in wreath. Copper. D. 85.

92 Same obverse. ℞ no figure in wreath. Brass.

93 MONROE ASSOCIATION, BALTO. ℞ "Good for 5 Cents." Brass. D. 86.

94 MONTEBELLO CLUB, BALTO. COUNTY. In centre figure "5." ℞ eagle. Brass. D. 87.

95 MOORE & BRADY, Baltimore. In centre rectangular space is relief. ℞ Liberty head. Brass. D. 88.

96 Same. ℞ counterstamped # 3 Y Brass.

96a MOORE & BRADY Five Baltimore. ℞ blank. D. 87.

97 MOUNT VERNON CLUB. "5" in centre. Rev. Liberty head. Brass.

98 NATIONAL BREWING CO. Balto. Co., Md. 1 Glass Beer. Brass. ℞ blank. Brass.

99 NONPAREIL, BALTIMORE. In center figure "5." ℞ Liberty head. Below head, "P. H. J." in small letters. Nickel. D. 91.

100 Same. Counterstamped "B. A." D. 91.

101 NEW YORK CLOTHING HOUSE. White metal. D. 90.

102 H. W. & SONS. ℞ Shield. Brass.

103 O'BRIEN'S 5 S. Liberty St. Baltimore. ℞ "2½" in very large figures. Brass. D. 92.

104 O'BRIEN'S 303 Second St. Balto. ℞ same as last. Nickel. D. 93.

105 O'BRIEN'S, 3 N. Calvert St. In centre, "2½." ℞ same as above obverse, incused. Nickel. Quatrefoil shape. D. 74.

106 O'NEILL & CO. *1* Gal. Canton. ℞ "Redeemable * From Shuckers * Only." Nickel. D. 95.

107 PATAPSCO FRUIT BUTTER COMPANY, No. 27 South Liberty St.

108 Baltimore, Md. ℞ Liberty Bell. Brass. D. 97.

109 Same. White metal. D. 97.

110 Same obverse. ℞ Independence Hall. White metal. D. 98.

111 Same. Brass.

112 Same obverse. ℞ Carpenter's Hall. White metal. D. 99.

113 Same obverse. ℞ Libertas Americana. White metal. D. 100.

114 Same obverse. ℞ Continental soldier. White metal. D. 101.

115 Same obverse. ℞ Maryland coat of arms. White metal. D. 102.

116 Same obverse. ℞ double head. White metal.

117 Same obverse. ℞ Public Bldg. White metal.

118 PETERS, W., BALTO. 1849. counterstamped on reverse of cent of 1838. D. 103.

119 PLATT & CO., BALTIMORE. In centre figure "5." over circle of rays. ℞ similar to obverse. Brass. D. 104.

120 Same obverse. ℞ Liberty head. Brass.

121 PLATT & CO. BALTO. In centre figure "3." ℞ same as obverse. Brass.

122   PRICE BROS. BALTIMORE. In centre, "1866." ℞ One Gallon Oysters. In centre an oyster. Nickel. D. 105.

123   PRICE BROS. & CO. Otherwise similar to last. Nickel. D. 106.

124   PRINGSHEIM, BALTIMORE. ℞ "One White." Brass. D. 107.

125   PYFER & CO. 1849. Liberty head. ℞ Eagle. Brass. D. 108.

126   Same. German silver. Very rare

127   RANDALL & CO. BALT. ℞ Mineral Water. City Hotel. German silver. Plain edge. D. 109.

128   Same. Reeded edge. German silver. D. 109.

129   REID, P. J., 65, (large figures.) All incuse. ℞ plain. Nickel. D. 110.

130   RULLMANN, W., WASHINGTON HALL. In centre, "One Drink." ℞ A lyre. Brass. D. 113.

131   RUTH, FRANCIS J. In centre "1 Gall." ℞ eagle. Brass. D. 114.

132   SAUTER, FRANK, 307 E. FAYETTE ST., BALTO MD. ℞ "5." D. 115. Aluminum.

133   SCHOFIELD, HENRY, HANOVER ST . 5c D. 116.

134   SCHUTZEN PARK, BALTO. In centre two crossed guns behind a target, surrounded by a wreath, a star above. ℞ a figure "5" in wreath, a star at the top. Brass. D. 117.

135   Same. Nickel. D. 117.

136   Same. as last, but figures "10." Brass. D. 118.

137   Same. Copper. D. 118.

138   Same obverse as last. Same reverse as last, but date "1875" above figure "5." D. 119.

139   Same as last, but figures "25." Brass. D. 120.

140   Same as last obverse. Reverse with date "1875" below figures "10." Copper.

141   SCHUETZEN PARK, BALTO. In centre two crossed guns above a target. No wreath. ℞ figure "5" in wreath, similar to first-mentioned variety, but from different die. Large stars. Brass. Same. Copper. Duffield 121.

142   Same obverse as last. ℞ same as reverse of first mentioned variety, with wreath points close to star. Brass.

143   Same as Duffield 121, but figures "10." Copper. D. 122.

144   Same as last, but figures "25." Nickel. D. 123.

145   SCHUTZEN PARK, BALTO. In centre the figures "10." ℞ a target with two crossed guns above, and two crossed branches below. Brass. D. 124.

146   Same, except with the figures "25." Brass. D. 125.

147   Same, except with the figures "100." Nickel. D. 126.

148   SEGER, JACOB, SILVER PLATER, &c. ℞ eagle. Brass. Plain edge. D. 127.

149   Same. Brass. Reeded edge. D. 127.

150   Same. Copper. Plain edge. D. 127.

151   Same. Copper. Reeded edge. D. 127.

152   Same. German silver. D. 127.

153   SHAKESPEARE CLUB, BALTO. In centre figure "5." ℞ Liberty head. Dated, 1863. Brass. D. 128.

154   Same as last, but figures "10" in centre. Brass.

155 SHRIVER, JOHN L., & BROS., 307 W. Pratt St. ℞ eagle. Brass. D. 130.

156· SMITH & WICKS, BALTO. Figure "5" in centre over a circle of rays. ℞ seated figure of Liberty. Brass. D. 134.

157 Same as last. Counterstamped "A. K." Brass. D. 134.

158 SEC. DEM. T. UNION. In centre figure "5." ℞ owl, &c. Brass. D. 135.

159 SOULSBY, ROBERT. A wreath inclosing "Voux Hall." ℞ eagle. "Baltimore" below. German silver. D. 136.

160 SPENCER, L. C., & CO. ℞ "One Gallon" above, with two crossed branches below. In centre an oyster. Nickel. D. 138.

161 SPENCER, L. C., & CO. Below, an ornament. In centre an oyster. ℞ (10 Galls) within a wreath, a star at the top. Nickel. D. 139.

162 STEINBACH, GEO. P., BALTIMORE ,MD. ℞ "Importer of Toys & Fancy Goods." Liberty head in centre in beaded circle. Copper. D. 140.

163 STEINBACH, GEO. P., BALTIMORE, MD. ℞ inscription same as last. This piece is of the size of a U. S. double eagle, and an imitation of the design of this coin. The first mentioned piece is of the size of a ten-dollar piece. Copper.

164 STEVENS, CHAS., 5 Cents in Goods. Brass. D. 141.

165 STROUSE & BROTHERS HIGH ART· CLOTHING, BALTIMORE & NEW YORK. ℞ blank. Aluminus. D. 142.

166 TEUTONIA CLUB, BALTO. CO. Figures "25" in wreath. Brass. D. 143.

167 TOLAND, WILLIAM. Brass, thin planchet. D. 144.

168 TAFELRUNDE DEUTSCHER MAENNER. BALTO. ℞ Good for 25 Cents." "KOEHLER" in small letters below. Brass.

169 Same obverse. ℞ some, but figure "5." Brass.

170 TRAUSCH, CHAS., BALTIMORE. In centre figure "5." ℞ Liberty head. Below, in small letters. "P. H. J." Brass. D. 145.

171 Same obverse. ℞ a flower with twelve petals. Lead. D. 146.

172 TURNER, ROBERT, & SON, on reverse of silver dollar of 1867. D. 147.

173 TWAITS, T. D., & CO. In centre an oyster. In exergue, a star ℞ "Baltimore, Md." Brass. D. 148.

174 U. S. MANF'G CO. STEEL STAMPS, STENCILS, &c., 97 W. Lombard ST., BALTIMORE. ℞ "Maryland Institute, 25th Exhibition Oct. 1872. Balto. Md. Nickel. D. 149.

175 Same. Brass.

176 Same as last. Counterstamped with a figure "5." D. 149.

177 U. B. V. in monogram. ℞ blank. Brass. D. 150.

178 WEIL, MORITZ H., 19 NORTH FREDERICK ST., BALTIMORE. ℞ "Good for 5 Cents." Brass. D. 151.

179 W. BALTO. SCHUETZEN PARK. In centre a target, with two crossed guns above. ℞ blank. Brass. D. 152.

180 WOODALL, WM. E., & CO. SHIP BUILDERS, BALTIMORE. ℞ a ship in dry dock. Brass. D. 153. Very rare.

181 YINGER, A. ELLICOTTS MILLS. ℞ an omnibus drawn by two horses. German silver. Oval. D. 154.
182 B. F. Z. & CO. CITIZENS LINE. ℞ "Omnibus." Nickel. Oval. D. 155.
183 Same. Counterstamped with figure "5." D. 155.

CRISFIELD.

184 GIBSON, (S. H.) & SON, OYSTER PACKERS. "I Gall." ℞ plain Brass. 25m. D. 50.
184a MILLIGAN (E. W.) & SON. "1 Gal." ℞ female head, 1875. Brass. 20m.

CUMBERLAND.

185 RINGGOLD, REINHART, Pharmacists. ℞ "Good for One 10c Glass of Soda. Aluminum. Reeded edge. 25m. D. 111.
186 Similar obverse. ℞ similar, but "5." Octagonal. Reeded edge. 25m. D. 112.

HAGERSTOWN.

187 BOWMAN, G. R., CONFECTIONER. ℞ a telescope and inscription. Brass. 22m. D. 14.
188 MacGILL & MOORE, with "5" in circle of rays. ℞ female head. Brass. 20m. D. 78.

WESTMINSTER.

189 SHRIVER (B. F.) & CO. In centre "5" in circle of rays. ℞ female head. German silver. 25m. D. 129.
190 Similar obverse, but "3" in centre. White metal. 20m.

WOODBERRY.

191 SOVEREIGNS OF INDUSTRY, EXCELSIOR COUNCIL No. 3. ℞ 1 counterstamped. ℞ female head. 1876. Brass. 25m. D. 137.

NOTE.—The reference D is to Mr. F. G. Duffield's list published in the Numismatist of 1907.

MASSACHUSETTS.

ATTLEBORO.

1 RICHARDS, H. M. & E. I., JEWELRY. ℞ Schenck's Patent Planing Machine. Copper . Low 164. Rare.
— 2 RICHARDS, H. M. & E. I. ℞ Lafayette standing. Copper. Low 83.

NOTE.—The Schenck Machine reverse also occurs with the cards of W. P. Haskins of Troy, N. Y., and Peck & Burnham of Boston.

— 3 SCHENCK, S. B., PLANING MACHINE. ℞ "Grooving or Jointing" &c.
Copper. Low 84.

BOSTON.

4 Apollo Garden, Hess & Speidel, Good for 6 Cents. 576 Washington St.
℞ Head of Apollo. Copper. 27m.
5 Same. White metal.
6 Same. White metal. Gilded.
7 Same obverse. White metal. Counterstamped "10."
8 Same obverse. Counterstamped "20." White metal.
9 Same obverse. ℞ Bust of Lincoln. Copper. Excessively rare.
10 Same obverse. White metal. Excessively rare.
11 Same obverse. ℞ card of George Fera, Studio Building. White metal.
12 Same obverse. ℞ Bust of Washington. White metal.
13 Same obverse. ℞ WASHINGTON THE FATHER OF OUR COUNTRY.
White metal.
14 Same obverse. ℞ Card of Chamberlain, Norfolk, Va. White metal.
15 Same obverse. ℞ MADE FROM COPPER TAKEN FROM THE RUINS
OF THE TURPENTINE WORKS NEWBERN, N. C. DESTROYED BY
THE REBELS MARCH 14, 1862. Copper. Rare.
16 Head of Apollo. ℞ PARTIES SUPPLIED, &c. Copper.
17 Same. White metal.
18 AYER, WELLS W., 146 Washington Street. ℞ blank. German silver.
32m.
19 BAKER, WRIGHT & HOWARD, LADIES SALOON, 81 COURT ST.
White metal. 27m.
20 BEALS, J. J. & W., CLOCKS. Face of a clock. Brass.
21 Same obverse. ℞ N. C. FOLGER, 17 OLD LEVEE. Copper.
22 Same obverse. ℞ GENTLEMAN'S FURNISHINGS, &c. Brass. Rare.
23 Same. Copper.
24 Same obverse. ℞ C. W. JACKSON, COAL DEALER. Copper.
25 Same obverse. ℞ Blank. Copper. Rare.
25a BRADFORD, M. L. & CO., 142 Wash St., Hardware. White metal.
26 CHASE, F. J. & CO., Boston. ℞ M. L. BRADFORD & CO. CUTLERY
AND HARDWARE. 27m. White metal.
27 COOK, HENRY, MONEY BROKER. Eagle on apothecary's mortar.
Copper. Excessively rare.
28 COOK, HENRY, NO SURRENDER OF THE FORT SUMTER OF THE
NORTH. Copper. 43m.
29 Same. White metal.
30 CURRIER & GREELEY. Eagle. ℞ NOT ONE CENT BUT JUST AS
GOOD. Copper. Plain edge.
31 Same as reverse of preceding. ℞ Heidsick & Fils, Rheims. Bunch of
grapes. Copper. Excessively rare, perhaps unique.
32 Same obverse. ℞ Piper & Co., Rheims. Grape leaves and grapes.
Copper. Excessively rare, perhaps unique.
33 Same obverse. ℞ GENTLEMAN'S FURNISHING STORE. Eagle.
Copper. Rare.

34 CONSULT DR. DARBY, BOSTON, counterstamped on Spanish two-real
   pieces.
35 DADMUN, F. W., & CO., 15 Court St., Massachusetts Eating House.
   White metal. 27m.
36 E. R. R. UP CHECK. Eastern Railroad Company. Brass. 21m.
37 Similar. DOWN CHECK. Brass. 21m.
38 FARNSWORTH, PHIPPS & CO Dealers in Dry Goods. Copper. Rare.
39 FERA, GEORGE, STUDIO BUILDING. ℞ PARTIES SUPPLIED AT
   SHORT NOTICE. Counterstamped "10." White metal.
40 Similar. Counterstamped "20." White metal.
41 Same obverse. ℞ Head of Apollo. White metal.
42 Same obverse. ℞ Soldiers' Fair, Springfield, &c. Copper. Very rare.
43 Same. White metal.
44 Same obverse. ℞ Hess & Speidel, Good for 6 cents. Copper. Rare.
45 JAMESON & VALENTINE, Spring Lane, Boston. White metal. (Levick 1714).
46 KENDALLS, BOSTON. (Levick 1716). White metal.
47 LEARNED & CO., Congress Street. (Levick 1716). White metal.
48 LOW, JOHN H. & CO. WATCHES, JEWELRY &c. Brass. 32m. Excessively rare. Only one specimen known.
49 MAHONYS' CLOTHING. Brass. Plain edge.
50 MARSTON, R., & CO. German silver. 25m. (Levick 1718.)
51 MARSTON, E., & CO. ℞ Pay at the Counter. Size 25m. White metal.
52 MAVERICK COACH. 1837. ℞ EAST BOSTON 1837. Feuchtwanger.
   metal. 18½m. Low 116.
52a Same. Copper.
53 MECHANICAL BAKERY. Brass.
54 MECHANICS SAVINGS BANK. ℞ PRESENT THIS CHECK. White
   metal. 27m.
55 MERRIAM, JOSEPH H. DIE CUTTER. ℞ Washington in wreath.
   Copper.
56 Same. Brass.
57 Same. White metal.
58 Same obverse. ℞ Lincoln. Copper. 32m.
59 Same oberse. ℞ Daniel Webster. Copper. 32m.
60 Same. Brass.
61 Same. White metal.
62 Same obverse. ℞ Albert Edward, Prince of Wales. Copper.
63 Same. Brass.
64 Same. White metal.
65 Same obverse. ℞ Bust of Merriam, LABOR OMNIA VICIT. Copper.
66 Same. Brass.
67 Same. White metal.
68 Same obverse. ℞ Bust of Thomas Sayers, Champion of England. 1859.
   Copper.

69 Same obverse. ℞ Bust of John C. Heenan, Champion of America
    1859. Copper.

70 MESSER, W. W., 212 WASHINGTON ST. ℞ PARTIES SUPPLIED &c.
    Counterstamped "30." White metal. 27m.

71 Similar. "28." White metal.

72 MILTON W. H., MERCHANT TAILOR, &c. Copper. FANUEIL HALL.

73 MILTON, WM. H. & CO., Clothing, FANEUIL HALL. Copper.

74 Similar to preceding, but from different die. Addition of small stars
    to right and left of the word WAREHOUSE, and omission of period
    after the word CLOTHING. Copper. (See "Numismatist," 1914,
    Page 65).

75 MILLIKEN'S HOTEL. Brass. 30m.

76 NEW ENGLAND DINING SALOON, 142 Wash. St., Boston, Mass. Cop-
    per.

77 Same obverse. ℞ Card of F. J. CHASE & CO. Brass. 27m. Figure
    stamped in centre.

78 Same obverse. ℞ Card of Jos. H. Merriam. 32m.

79 NOWLIN & McELWAIN, JEWELERS. ℞ Clock face, &c. White
    metal. (Levick 1728).

80 PECK & BURNHAM, Dry Goods, Copper.

81 Same obverse. ℞ Schenck's Planing Machine. Copper.

82 PERKINS, E., Congress Street. Reverse same as obverse. Stamped
    "30." White metal. 27m.

83 Similar. ℞. Perkins & Co. Congress St. White metal. 27m.

84 PORTER, HORACE, WATCHES. Brass. Same. Silvered planchet.

85 REUTER & ALLEY, HIGHLAND SPRING BREWERY. Brass. Ex-
    cessively rare. (See Numismatist, 1914, Page 453).

86 Same. Silvered planchet. Excessively rare.

87 ROXBURY COACHES. ℞ NEW LINE 1837. Feuchtwanger metal.
    18½m. Low 129.

88 RUTTER, WILLIAM. Old Rags, Junk, &c. Copper. (See "Numis-
    matist," 1915, Page 143).

89 SAMPSON, Z. S. ICE CREAM SODA. Soda fountain. White metal.

90 STANWOOD, H. B., & CO., WATCHES, JEWELRY, &c. Brass. 19m.

91 TUTTLE C. F., 130 WASHINGTON ST. "16" in centre. ℞ Head of
    Washington to right. White metal. 27m.

92 Same. Brass.

93 VINTON, C. A. 212 Washington St. "12" in centre. ℞ Same as ob-
    verse. White metal. 27m.

94 WHITE BROS. & CO. ℞ Horse Shoe. Copper.

95 WILLARD, ALFRED. Brushes, etc. Comb in field. Copper. See
    Numismatist 1914, page 148.

96 WRIGHT S. & CO. White metal.

NEW BEDFORD.

99 BRIGHAM, FRANCIS L. Dry Goods. A long low building. Single border of dots. Copper. Low 73.
100 Same dies probably retouched. Double border of dots. Copper. Low 72. Very rare.

SPRINGFIELD.

101 BOLEN, J. A. Die Sinker and Medallist. 1862. ℞ Boy on eagle. Copper. 75 struck.
102 Same. Brass. 75 struck.
103 BOLEN, J. A. 1864. Bust. ℞ Liberty cap, with sunburst. Oroide. 25 struck.
105 Similar. Smaller date. ℞ STAMP CUTTER, DIE SINKER, etc. Copper. 25 struck.
106 BOLEN, J. A. 1865. Bust. ℞ Same as preceding. Copper. 10 struck.
107 Same. White metal. 10 struck.
108 Similar, on obverse TWO STRUCK & DIE DESTROYED. White metal. 2 struck.
109 BOLEN, J. A. 1865. Bust. ℞ Laurel wreath, DIE SINKER, etc. Small "B" under MASS. Oroide. 50 struck.
110 Same. White metal. 50 struck.
111 Head of Bolen to left. J. A. BOLEN. Under bust BOLEN. The only Bolen card with name under bust. ℞ DIE SINKER, &c. Same as _. Bolen 21. Silver. 1 struck.
112 Same. Copper. 15 struck.
113 Same. Brass. 15 struck.
114 Same. White metal. 15 struck.
115 BOLEN, J. A. 1867. Bust ℞ Libertas Americana. Silver. 1 struck. Bolen 32.
116 Same. Brass. 1 struck.
117 BOLEN, J. A. 1869. Bust. ℞ Same as preceding. Bolen 217. Silver. 1 struck.
118 Same. Copper. 28 struck.
119 Same. Brass. 20 struck.
120 Same. White metals. 50 struck.
121 Same. White metal. 3 struck.
122 Same. Copper. 16 struck.
123 BOLEN, J. A. 1869. Bust. ℞ View of old Pynchon House. Silver. 10 struck.
124 Same. Copper. 95 struck.
125 Same. Brass. 45 struck.
126 MOORE BROTHERS. PHOTOGRAPHIC ARTISTS. Copper. Only 5 struck.
127 Same. Brass. Only 1 struck.
128 Same. White metal. 400 struck.
129 TILLY HAYNES & CO. EXHIBITION OF CLOTHING &c. View of Crystal Palace, London, 1851. Copper. Very rare.
130 Same. White metal. Very rare.

TAUNTON.

131 ADAMS, JOHN J. Brushes. A hog. Copper.
132 Same. Brass.
-133 CROCKER BROS. & CO. Zinc and copper nails, etc. Copper.
134 Same. Zinc or white metal.
135 STRANGE, E. W. STEEL LETTER CUTTER. Eagle. 23m head. Very rare.
136 HUNTLEY, A. Head 23m. Very rare.

MICHIGAN.

DETROIT.

1 BROWN BROS. CIGAR MAKERS. GOOD FOR ONE **FONTELLA** CIGAR. Copper.
2 DIMMICK, J. Jewelry. Eagle. Copper. Plain edge.
3 Same. Brass. Milled edge.
4 TYLER, C. C. & CO. BOOTS & SHOES. Copper.
5 Same. Brass.
6 Same. Silvered planchet.

GRAND RAPIDS.

7 BALL, DANIEL & CO. Foreign exchange. Eagle. ℞ Safe opens to r. Brass.
8 Same. Safe opens to l. Brass.
9 Similar. Eagle's wing before D in DANIEL. Brass.
10 FOSTER & PARRY, HARDWARE, STOVES, etc. Stove. ℞ Padlock. Brass.
11 Same. Copper.
11a
NOTE.—There are minor die varieties of the above.
12 FOSTER, MARTIN & CO. HARDWARE. Anvil. ℞ Stove. Brass.

MISSISSIPPI.

SILVER LAKE.

1 JEWELL, J. D., 25 Cents. White metal. 20m.

VICKSBURG.

2 CROOM & HILL, HOTEL DIXIE. ℞ 50. German silver. 30m.
3 FOTTERALL, BENJN. F. Fancy Goods. Eagle. Copper. Plain edge.
4 Same. Brass. Milled edge.
5 Same obverse. ℞ Three umbrellas. Richardson card of Philadelphia. A mule. Brass. Rare.
6 Same obverse. ℞ Eagle on mortar. A mule. Copper.
7 Same obverse. ℞ WATCHES, CLOCKS, etc. A mule. Brass. **Rare.**
8 Same obverse. ℞ Locomotive head light, Olcott card of Rochester, N. Y. A mule. Brass. Rare.
9 Same. White metal.

MISSOURI.

ST. LOUIS.

1   ANHEUSER-BUSCH BREW'G ASS'N. ℞ an eagle. 1880. Copper.
2   BURROWS & JENNINGS. 1836. GROCERIES. WINES. SHIP CHAN-
    DLERY. Brass. Low. 102. Ex. rare.
3   Same. White metal. Low 102. Ex. rare.
4   BOHANNAN, DR., MEDICAL OFFICE, 63 PINE ST. ℞ inscription
    in eleven lines. White metal. Only one specimen known. (Betts
    sale No. 179.)
5   COHN, M. A., 68 W. —th ST. ℞ blank. Brass.
6   COX, M. B., & CO., WHOLESALE DEALERS IN HATS & CAPS.
    Eagle in field. Copper.
7   HUCKEL, BURROWS & JENNINGS. 1836. GROCERIES, WINES,
    SHIP CHANDLERY. Brass, silvered. Low 177. Excessively rare.
    Same. White metal. Low 178. Excessively rare.
8   JACCARD, E., & CO. Shield. Brass.
9   Same. Copper.
10   Same. White metal.
11   Same. Silver. Rare.
12   LONG, E. DAGUERROTYPES. Liberty head. ℞ eagle. Brass.
13   Same obverse. ℞ Foster & Parry token, Grand Rapids. A padlock.
    Copper.
14   Same. White metal.
15   Same. Brass, plain edge.
16   Same. Brass, reeded edge.
17   LONG, H. H., 3RD & MARKET ST. Brass. Reeded edge.
18   Same. Brass. Plain edge. Very thick planchet.
19   Same. White metal. Thick planchet.
20   MANVILL, S. 25 cent tokens. Lead.
21   NICHOLSON'S GROCERY. 1850. Eagle. ℞ Fitzgibbons. Copper,
    plain edge.
22   Same. Brass. Reeded edge.
23   NICHOLSON'S HALF DIME TOKEN. An eagle. 15m.
24   NICHOLSONS. Scales. ℞ STATE OF MISSOURI HALF DIME. 15m.
25   NICHOLSONS HALF DIME. 20 GOOD FOR A DOLLAR. White
    metal. 15m.
26   PEASE, J. S., & CO. HARDWARE. ℞ Anvil, arm with sledge, card
    of L. G. Irving, New York. Brass. Excessively rare.
27   PROUHET, H. Incused on reverse, "148." Copper. 31m. Very rare.
28   SANDERS, C. G., DEALER IN WOOD, COAL & KINDLING. Wagon
    drawn by four mules. White metal. 25m.
29   ST. LOUIS POST OFFICE. Eagle on shield. ℞ (Edwill & Berry)
    White metal. Extremely rare. 25m.
30   ST. LOUIS POST OFFICE. Eagle. ℞ STATE SAVINGS ASS in en-
    graved letters. Copper. 28m.
31   Same obverse. ℞ CLAFLIN, ALLEN & CO. Copper.
32   Same obverse. ℞ LEPERE & RICHARD. Engraved by J. M. Ker-
    shaw. White metal. 24m.

33 Same obverse. ℞ HUME & CO. Copper. 28m. Engraved by Stub-
    enrough & Weber.
34 Same obverse. ℞ SCOTT & BROS. Copper.
35 Same obverse. ℞ W. & H. V. Copper.
36 SWOPE, JOEL. SHOES. ℞ Continental Soldier. Brass.
37 VAN-DEVENTER, J. & W., & CO., CLOTHING. Eagle. Silver, thick
    planchet. Excessively rare.
38 VAN-DEVENTER, J. & W. Silver, thin planchet. Excessively rare.
39 Same. Brass.

INDEPENDENCE.

40 ABRAHAMS, M. A., OUTFITTING STORE. Head of Washington.
    Brass.

WESTON.

41 ABRAHAMS, M. A. Type of preceding. Brass.

KANSAS CITY.

42 SMITH & RIEGER, HATTERS. 5 Cents. Brass. Very rare.

NEW HAMPSHIRE.

DOVER.

1   SMITH, A. C., CROCKERY, GLASSWARE, &c. ℞ HASELTON &
    PALMER, DRY GOODS GROCERIES, &c. Copper. Low 131.

NASHUA.

2   ROBY, N. W., ENGINEER FOR ROGERS & SON, NASHUA, N. H. ℞
    Eagle. Brass. 27m. Said to be unique.

PORTSMOUTH.

3   MARCH, NATH'L, BOOKSELLER & STATIONER. ℞ WILLIAM
    SIMES & CO., TEAS, WINES, & GROCERIES. Copper. Low 124.
4   SISE E. F., & CO., COMMISSION MERCHANTS, COAL, &c. Copper.
    Low 132.
5   SISE, E. F. & CO. The above dies used on a Spanish half real, neces-
    sarily only a portion of the lettering showing. Silver. Unique.

NEW JERSEY

BELLEVILLE.

1   BERGEN IRON WORKS. 1840. Eagle with spread wings. ℞ Clasped
    hands. Brass. (Low 142).

2 Similar. Inferior dies. Circles instead of stars on obverse. Copper (Low 143.)
3 Same. Brass.

(The two preceding frequently come with broken dies.)

— 4 DUSEAMAN, T. BUTCHER. Eagle. ℞ Bouquet. Copper. (Low 148).
5 GIBBS, J., MANUFACTURER. Ship. Copper. (Low 150.)
6 GIBBS, W., AGRICULTURIST. ℞ Steer in centre of field. Copper. (Low 151.) Rare.
7 HOWELL WORKS GARDEN. Bunch of grapes. ℞ SIGNUM 1834. Copper. (Low 81.)
8 HOWELL WORKS GARDEN. A rose. ℞ TOKEN. Copper. (Low 163.)
9 SEAMAN, T. D., BUTCHER. ℞ Same as Low 66, a cow. Copper. (Low 155.)

GLASSBORO.

10 BODINE BROS. 1856. ONE CENT DUE BEARER IN MDZE AT COUN-TER OF OUR STORE. ℞ Blank. Brass. 27m.
11 BODINE BROTHERS. Similar to foregoing, but different date. "1863." Brass. 27m.
— 12 WARRICK & STANGER. 1872. "1 CENT DUE BEARER IN MDZE AT OUR STORE." Brass. 19m.
13 Same. Nickel.
14 Same. White metal.
15 Same. Copper.
16 WHITNEY, S. A. 1852. ONE CENT. Brass. 27m.
17 Same. Silver. Very rare.
18 WHITNEY GLASS WORKS. DUE BEARER ONE CENT. 1869. Sil-ver. 19m. Rare.
19 Same. Copper.
— 20 Same. Brass.
21 Same. White metal, thin planchet.
22 Same. White metal, thick planchet.

MOUNT HOLLY

23 SHREVE, ALFRED R. DEALER IN HARDWARE, PAINTS, OILS, &c. Brass.
24 Same. Copper.
25 Same. White metal.

NEWARK.

26 ALLERS, GEORGE. Clock face. Copper. Rare.
27 BARNETTS MALLEABLE AND GREY IRON. Made of cast iron. Rare.

28 BRAGAW, E. & I., NEWARK AND MOBILE, ALA.   HAT MFGS.
    Copper. Excessively rare.
29 Same. Brass. Excessively rare.
30 Same. White metal or composition. Excessively rare.

NORTH BEACH HAVEN.

31 GUARANTEE DEVELOPMENT CO. struck on Spanish 2 reals of 1722.
    Silver. Ex. rare.

TRENTON

32 KENNEDY, S. Eagle on shield. ℞ shield, SLATER WALTON & CO.
    PHILA. White metal, 22m. (Said to have been but eight struck.)
33 PINE, G., TRENTON, N. J. ℞ similar to United States quarter dollar.
    24m. Electrotype silvered. Rare.

NEW YORK.

ALBANY.

1 FOWLER, H. G., DRUGGIST, 109 GENESEE ST. Copper. Excessively rare.
2 D. CHURCH PENNY. ℞ Plain (FIRST PRESBYTERIAN CHURCH
   1790). Copper. V. Rare.
— 3 MEADE & BROTHER, DAUGERRIAN GALLERIES EXCHANGE
   ALBY. ℞ eagle. Brass.
4 SAFFORD, N., TEMPERANCE HOUSE, 280 NORTH MARKET ST.
   Copper.
5 Same. White metal.

BATAVIA.

6 COCHRAN, J., BELLFOUNDER, BATAVIA. Copper. (Low 161.) Ex.
   rare.

BROOKLYN.

7 ROLLER SKATING ASSOCIATION. 1876. Skate in field. ℞ BROOK-
   LYN RINK SKATE CHECK. Brass. 15¼m. Rare.
8 Same. ℞ McCORMICK'S PARK SKATE CHECK. Copper. Rare.
9 COGAN, EDWARD. White metal.
10 Same. Silver. Rare.
11 KNAPP. ℞ blank. Nickel. 24½. Rare.
12 LEASK. 6 SANDS ST., LACE, EMBROIDERIES, etc. White metal. 19.
-13 CONEY ISLAND ELEPHANT. View of elephant. Brass.
-14 Same. Copper.
15 Same. White metal.
16 CROWN STEAM LAUNDRY, 474 MYRTLE AVE., BROOKLYN. ℞
    blank. Brass.

CHITTENANGO.

27 ROBINSON, L. MANUFACTURER OF COMPOUND MAGNETS. Copper. Reeded edge. Rare.
28 Same. Nickel. Rare.
29 Same. White metal. Rare.

HUDSON.

30 CLARK, JAMES, & CO., CLOTHING MANUFACTURERS. View of building on obverse. Brass. Reeded edge.
31 Same. ℞ similar, but word spelled "CLOTING." Brass. Plain edge.
32 Same. ℞ same as reverse of Doremus & Dixon, with ship in field. Brass. Plain edge.
33 Same. ℞ same as reverse of West's Ministrels, the New York Crystal ·Palace. Copper. Plain edge.

JAMESTOWN.

34 SHARPE, A. D., PEOPLES DRY GOODS STORE. ℞ Bust of James G. BLAINE. Brass. 15m.

LANSINGBURGH.

35 WALSH'S GENERAL STORE, &c. ℞ plow, and inscription. Copper. (Low 99.)
— 36 Same. ℞ standing figure of Lafayette. Copper. (Low 100.)
37 Similar to foregoing, but word spelled "LANSINBURGH," in straight line. Copper. (Low 101.)

LONG ISLAND.

38 RAHMING, EDWIN. Brass. 13m. Ex. Rare.

MIDDLETOWN.

39 BAKEWELL & CO. W. M. & B. MIDDLETOWN, N. Y. ℞ blank.
Brass. 27m. Ex. Rare.

MORRISANIA.

40 RIVINIUS, C. Brass. 16m. Rare.

NEW YORK CITY.

41 ADMIT. ℞ 1817. Copper. Admission token to old Park Theatre.
42 ALEXANDER, HERR. 1847. His bust to r. Brass. by C. C. W.
43 ANDERSON, HENRY, BOOTS & SHOES. ℞ A boot. Copper. Low
107.
44 ASHTON, S. AMERICAN INN, CANAL ST. Rare. Brass. ℞ 3D.
45 ATWOOD'S RAILROAD HOTEL, 243 BROADWAY. Three Cent Token.
Equestrian figure of Washington, BALE & SMITH below. ℞ CARRY
ME TO ATWOODS, etc. Copper. Rare and one of the most interesting early New York Cards.
46-47 Same. Brass. Very rare.
48 Same. White metal. Rare.
49 AUSTIN C., ENGRAVER. An elephant. Brass. Extremely rare. 317.
50 BAILLY, WARD & CO., Importers, 41 Maiden Lane. White metal. Extremely rare.
51 BALE & SMITH, Engravers & Die Cutters, 68 Nassau St. Equestrian
figure of Washington as on No. 6. Copper. Rare.
52 Same. White metal. Rare.
53 Similar. B. & S. below figure. Copper. Rare.
54 Same. White metal. Rare.
55 BALTIMORE & OHIO R. R. Horseshoe. Inscription. Brass.
56 BANCROFT, REDFIELD & RICE. NEW YORK between ornamental
dashes . ℞ Blank. Lead. ery rare.
57 BARKER, JOHN. AMERICAN REPOSITORY OF FINE ARTS. Head
of Washington in wreath. Brass. Very rare.
58 BARNUM'S MUSEUM. View of the building. ℞ Bust of Barnum and
list of attractions. Copper. Ex. Rare.
59 Same. White metal.
60 BENZIGER ZROS. RELIGIOUS ORNAMENTS, MEDALS, ETC. Brass.
LEAD.
61 BLACK, S. H. ELECTROTYPER, 1858. 390½ Broadway. Head of
Liberty. Electrotype (copper over lead)
62 Same. Silver over lead. Extremely rare.
63 BLACK, S. H. 1859. 410 BROADWAY. Electrotype (copper over
lead).
64 BLACK, S. H. 1859. 43 LISPENARD ST. Electrotype (copper over
lead).

65 BLACK, FRIEND &. (Placed here on account of similiarity of token)
    1860. 25 HOWARD ST. Electrotype (copper over lead).
66 BLACK, SAMUEL H. 1860. 142 ELM ST. Date is large. Electro-
    type (copper over lead).
67 BLACK, SAMUEL H. 1860 Small date. ℞ NO CENT in wreath. Elec-
    trotype (copper over lead).
68 BLACK, SAMUEL H. 1861 142 ELM ST. Electrotype (copper over
    lead).
69 BOLLENHAGEN, THEODOR & CO. Head of Liberty. ℞ City Hall,
    N. Y. Brass. Imitation of $20 gold piece.
70 Same type. Brass. Size of $10 gold piece.
71 Same type. Brass. Size of $5 gold piece.
72 Same type. Brass. Size of $2½ gold piece.
73 BONDY BROTHERS & CO. BELT MANUFACTURERS. Eagle. ℞
    Blank. Brass. Very rare.
74 BONDY BROTHERS & CO. BELT MANUFS. NEW YORK. Struck
    around the obverse of a U. S. cent of 1851. Extremely rare.
75 BOWEN & McNAMEE. SILK GOODS. 16 William St. Eagle. Brass.
76 Same. Copper.
77 Similar. Differing dies. 16 William St. Cor. Beaver. Brass.
78 Same. Copper.
79 JAS. S. BRADLEY, GILDER & FRAME MAKER, 154 WM. ST., N. Y.
    Stamped on U. S. quarter dollar, 1806. Very rare .
80 BRADSTREET, J. M. & SONS, MERCANTILE AGENCY. 1860. ℞
    BRADSTREET, HOFFMAN & CO. Collectors of Claims. Silver.
    Rare.
81 Same. Copper.
82 Same. Brass.
83 BREWSTER, J. & L. HAT MFG'S, 66 Water St. and 59 Chartres St.
    New Orleans. W. & B. N. Y. on reverse. Copper, gilt.
84 Same. Brass.
85 Similar. Differing dies. BALE, N. Y. on reverse . Copper, gilt.
86 Same. Brass.
87 BRIMELOW, T., DRUGGIST, 432 THIRD AVE. 1863. Head of Wash-
    ington to r. ℞ Pestle. Silver.
88 Same. German silver.
89 Same. Copper.
90 Same. Nickel.
91 Same. Nickel.
92 Same. White metal.
93 Same obverse. ℞ GOOD FOR ONE GLASS OF SODA. Silver.
94 Same. German silver.
95 Same. Copper.
96 Same. Brass.
97 Same. Nickel.
98 Same. White metal.
99 Same obverse. ℞ Bust of Franklin. Silver.
100 Same. Copper.
101 Same. Brass.

102 Same. Nickel.
103 Same. White metal.
104 Bust of Franklin. ℞ Pestle. Silver'
105 Same. Copper.
106 Same. Brass.
107 Same. Nickel.
108 Same. White metal.
109 Same obverse. ℞ GOOD FOR ONE CLASS OF SODA. Silver.
110 Same. Copper.
111 Same. Brass.
112 Same. Nickel.
113 Same. White metal.
114 Pestle. ℞ Same as preceding. Silver.
115 Same. Copper.
116 Same. Brass.
117 Same. Nickel.
118 Same. White metal.
119 Smaller head of Washington to l. ℞ Pestle. Silver.
120 Same. Copper.
121 Same. Brass.
122 Same. Nickel.
123 Same. White metal.
124 Same obverse. ℞ 2 in wreath. Silver.
125 Same. Copper.
126 Same. Brass.
127 Same. Nickel.
128 Same. White metal.
129 BRIMELQW, T. 1864. Head of Washington. ℞ Pestle. Silver.
130 Same. Copper.
131 Same. Brass.
132 Same. Nickel.
133 Same. Copper-nickel.
134 BROWN, H. & CO., CLOTHING. 314 Grand St. ℞ Bell. White metal. 16m.
135 Same obverse. ℞ Lincoln by Bolen. White metal. 26m.
136 Same obverse. ℞ Flag. White metal.
137 BUCHAN, DAVID C., CHAIR MFG. in field. "Northmore & Greenwich St." Brass. Rare.
138 Same. Silvered.
139 Similar. "Northmoore." Brass.
140 BUCKINGHAM PALACE ADMISSION TICKET. Brass.
141 BYRNE, ELEANOR RUGG. Bust to r. ℞ BYRNEORE GOLD 1859. Copper.
142 Same. Brass.
143 Same. White metal.
144 CARRINGTON & CO., 78 BROADWAY. The Havana Express. Horseman to r. Silver.
145 Same. Copper.
146 Same. Brass.

147 Same   White metal.

148 CENTRE MARKET, 14th Ward, N. York. Head of Liberty.   ℞ Market.
   Low 110. Copper.

149 Similar. Differing head. Low 111. Copper.

150 CHESEBROUGH, STEARNS & CO., Silk Goods. 37 Nassau St.   ℞
   Eagle. Ornamental dash over 37 and ornaments at either side, ornaments at ST. and dash below. Copper.

151 Same. Brass.

152 Same. Brass, silvered.

153 Similar. Without ornaments and dashes. Copper.

154 Same. Brass.

155 Obverse with ornaments and dashes.   ℞ DR. SELLECK above eagle.
   Copper.

156 Same. Brass.

157 CHISEBROUGH, STEARNS & CO. 37 "NASSAU ST."   ℞ Eagle. Ornaments and dashes on obverse. Brass.

158 Similar. Ornaments are larger. Brass.

159 CLARK, T. L., 247 Grand St., Brass checks, cards, etc. Brass. Betts
   sale. No. 48. Very rare.

160 CLARK, JAMES & CO. View of Building.   ℞ Importer and Jobbers of
   Fancy Dry Goods, 180 Broadway, New York. W. M. Rare.

161 CLINTON LUNCH. Bust in armor to l. ℞ Eagle . Brass. Very rare.

162 Same. German silver. Rare.

163 COLLINS READY MADE LINEN & FANCY STORE. Ship at wharf.
   Brass. Extremely rare.

164 COLUMBIA GARDEN. Star. ℞ Eagle. Lead. Rare.

165 COLUMBIA GARDEN. EBLING'S COLUMBIAN GARDEN 200 BOW-
   ERY, N. Y. stamped on Spanish two real piece. Very rare.

166 COOPER UNION. Reading Room Exit Ticket. Brass shell.

167 CROSSMAN, H. UMBRELLAS. 92½ Chatham St. Crude Liberty
   head. ℞ Umbrella. Copper. Low 112.

168 CROSSMAN, H. Eagle. ℞ Umbrella. Copper. Low 113.
   ℞ W. D. C. incuse. German silver. 19m. Extremely rare.

169 CRUMBIE, W. D., Cor of Bowery & Houston St. Soda Water Check.

170 Same. ℞ Plain.

171 CURTIS, JOHN K., WATCHMAKER and JEWELER. Head of Washington. Silver. Rare.

172 Same. Copper.

173 Same. Brass.

174 Same. White metal.

175 Similar. Bust of John Allan. Silver. Rare.

176 Same. Copper.

177 Same. Brass.

178 Same. White metal.

179 Similar. The Antiquary. Silver. Rare.

180 Same. Copper.

181 Same. Brass.

182 Same. White metal.

183 Mule. Bust of John Allan. ℞ The Antiquary. Silver. Rare.

184 Same. Copper.

185 Same. Brass.
186 Same. White metal.
187 Mule. The Antiquary. R The Great Eastern. White metal.
188 Same. Brass.
189 Same. Copper.
190 DAY, NEWELL & DAY. 589 Broadway. Copper. Rare.
191 Same. Brass. Rare.
192 Same. Feuchtwanger metal. Very rare.
193 DAYTON, J. H. STEAM WASHING ESTAB. 17th St. near 5th Ave. Head of Liberty. Copper. Low 114. Scarce.
194 DEAN, 17 UNION SQ. Cakes and Confectionery. Inscription in two curved lines. R Liberty head. White metal.
195 Same. R Carpenter's Hall. Copper.
196 Same. R Liberty bell. White metal.
197 Same. R Continental soldier. White metal.
198 Same. Copper.
199 Same. R Maryland arms. White metal.
200 Same. R Independence Hall. Copper.
201 Similar. Inscription in one straight and four curved lines. R Liberty head. White metal.
202 Same. R Liberty bell. White metal.
203 Same. R Continental soldier. White metal.
204 Same. Copper.
205 Same. R Maryland arms. White metal.
206 Same. R Independence Hall. Copper.
207 DELMONICO, 112 BROADWAY. 15 in centre. Brass.
208 DEVEAU, P. B. & S. 156 CHATHAM SQ. Boots & Shoes. Liberty head. R Boot. Copper. Low 115.
209 DODGE, J. SMITH, DENTIST, 407 Fourth St. R Eagle. Brass.
— 210 DOUGHERTY, PHILIP A. 1859. Liberty head. R GOOD FOR 6 CTS. Lead, copper plated. Copy of cent of this year. Scarce.
211 DOREMUS, SUYDAM & NIXON, 209 Pearl St. Dry Goods, N-York. Period after NIXON. Copper. Rare.
— 212 Same. Brass. Rare.
213 Similar. N. YORK. No period after NIXON. Copper. Rare.
214 Same. Brass. Rare.
215 Similar. W. & B. N. Y. on obverse R LINENS SHEETINGS & DA-MASKS in centre. Copper. Rare.
216 Same. Brass. Rare
217 DOREMUS, SUYDAM & NIXON. Name on obverse and reverse, by BALE, N. Y. 50 & 52 William St. Brass. Rare.
218 Similar. Hyphen between NEW and YORK. Brass. Rare.
— 219 DOREMUS, SUYDAM & NIXON, 39 Nassau, cor. Liberty St. Name on either side. In centre of reverse—DRY GOODS NEW YORK. Brass. Rare.
220 Similar. 37 & 39 Nassau St. B. & S. N. Y. Copper. Rare.
221 Same. Brass. Rare.
— 222 Similar 39 Nassau St. Cor. Liberty. Opp. the P. O. R DRY GOODS FOR HOTELS, STEAM BOATS & SHIPS. Copper.

223 Same. Brass.
224 DOREMUS & NIXON, 21 Park Place. Sailing vessel. ℞ Steamer.
     Copper.
225 Same. Brass.
226 Same. Brass, silvered.
227 Same. ℞ N. Y. Crystal Palace, 1853. Copper.
228 Same. ℞ War of 1861. Eagle United States Brass. Rare.
229 Same. ℞ War of 1812. Copper. Rare.
230 DRUIDICAL EXHIBITION. Admit Token. ℞ Eagle. Brass.
231 EHRET, GEORGE. Liberty head. ℞ 1 GLASS. Brass. 23m.
232 EVENING * NEWS—20 ℞ 20 enclosed in wreath 23m lead. Very Rare.
233 EICHLER, JOHN. Same type. Brass. 23m.
234 FARMERS & MECHANICS LIFE INSURANCE CO. Silver.
235 Same. Brass.
236 Same. Copper.
237 Same. White metal.
238 FEMALE PREVENTATIVE. Amulet. Liberty head in circle, border
     of stars. Brass. Rare.
239 Same. White metal. Rare.
240 FEUCHTWANGER, Dr. L. American Silver Composition. 377 Broad-
     way. Feuchtwanger metal. Very rare.
241 Similar but No. 2 Cortland St. Feuchtwanger composition. Very rare.
242 Feuchtwanger's Three Cent Token. 1837. Large eagle to l. ℞
     THREE CENTS in continuous wreath. Feuchtwanger composition.
     Low 118. Very rare.
243 Same. Copper. Excessively rare.
244 Similar type. Smaller eagle to l. ℞ 3 THREE CENTS in oak wreath.
     Feuchtwanger composition. Low 119. Very rare.
245 Three Cents. 1864. Facing eagle with spread wings. ℞ Same as
     preceding. Feuchtwanger metal. Scarce.
246 Three Cents. Arms of New York. ℞ THREE CENTS two rosettes
     and four stars in wreath. Low 117. Feuchtwanger composition.
247 Feuchtwanger Cent. 1837. Eagle to r. ℞ ONE CENT in wreath.
     Feuchtwanger metal. Low 120. There are many die varieties of
     this piece.
248 FIELD, W. HATTER. Hat in field. ℞ Beaver. Copper. Scarce.
249 FIFTH WARD MUSEUM HOTEL. ℞ 2/6. Brass. Very Rare.
250 FINCH, SANDERSON & CO., 8th Avenue Lines. ℞ An omnibus.
     TRANSFER TICKET. Lead. Scarce.
251 FINCK'S HOTEL. 6 in centre. Brass.
252 Similar. 9 in centre. Brass.
253 Same. Copper.
254 Similar. 12 in centre. Brass.
255 Similar. 15 in centre. Brass.
256 Same. Silver.
257 Similar. 18 in centre. Brass.
258 Similar. 21 in centre. Brass.
259 Similar. 24 in centre. Brass.
260 Same. Silver.

261 Similar. 30 in centre. Brass.

262 Same. Copper.

263 FITZGIBBON DAGUERREOTYPE GALLERY. Eagle. ℞ N. Y. Crystal Palace. Brass.

264 Same. Copper.

265 FRANCIS, PATENT SCREW. 399 & 402 Water St. Brass. Excessively rare.

266 FRANKLIN & CO. Union Square. Boys and Childrens Outfitting. ℞ Liberty bell. White metal.

267 Same. ℞ Lincoln by Bolen. Copper.

268 FREDERICK'S PHARMACY, 60th St. & Tnd Ave. Soda check. ℞ Liberty head. White metal.

269 Same. ℞ Liberty bell. White metal.

270 Same. ℞ Public Buildings. Copper.

271 Same. ℞ Continental soldier. White metal.

272 Same. Copper.

273 Same. ℞ two heads. Copper.

273a Same. ℞ Maryland arms. White metal.

274 Same. ℞ Capitol. Copper.

275 FRENCH'S HOTEL. German silver. 20m. Rare .

276 FURLONG, E. P. St. Patrick's Salve. ℞ St. Patrick. Brass.

277 GIBBS, J. NEW YORK-BELLEVILLE U S M STAGE. ℞ GOOD FOR ONE RIDE. Brass. Extremely rare.

278 GIBBS, W. AGRICULTURIST. Bouquet. ℞ Steer. Copper. Low 151. Very rare.

279 GIROUD, INVENTOR. ℞ Blank. German silver. Ex. Rare.

280 GLOBE FIRE INSURANCE CO. Globe. ℞ Liberty bell. Brass.

281 Same. Copper.

282 Same. White metal.

283 Same obverse. ℞ American flag. Copper.

284 Same. Brass.

285 Same. ℞ Lincoln by Bolen. White metal.

286 GOSLING'S RESTAURANT, 306 Broadway. Brass.

287 GOULD D. H., BOARDING & LODGINGS, 10 Fulton St. Liberty head. ℞ Eagle. Brass.

288 GREEN & WETMORE, HARDWARE, ETC. Cor. of Washington & VESEY Sts. ℞ Anvil. Brass. Plain edge.

289 Same. Reeded edge.

290 Same obverse. ℞ Hardware implements. Copy of card of T. S. Brown & Co.; Montreal. White metal. Very rare.

291 GRIMSHAW, W. D. THOS. PROSSER & SON. 15 Gold St. ℞ Stamping press.

292 HALLOCK & BATES, 234 Pearl St. Corner of Burling Slip. ℞ Similar to obverse with WHOLE SALE DRY GOODS below. Brass.

293 Obverse reverse of preceding. ℞ Blank. Brass.

294 HALLOCK, DOLSON & BATES, 41 William St. Dry Goods. Brass.

295 HARDIE, A. W. DRAPER AND TAYLOR, Cor. of Garden & William Sts. ℞ "Naked and ye Clothed Me." Brass .

296 HART, SAMUEL & CO. Playing Cards, 1 Barclay St. Jack of Clubs.
     ℞ 236 S. 56 St., Phila. Queen of Diamonds. Copper.
297 Same. White metal.
298 HART, SAMUEL & CO., Club House Cards. ℞ CARD COUNTER. 307
     B'way, New York, 416 So. Thirteenth St., Phila. Brass.
299 Same. Silvered.
300 HART & CO. A hand of cards with ace of hearts in centre. ℞
     similar with king of hearts in centre. Copper.
301 HASKINS & WILKINS. 4th Ave Line. ℞ TRANSFER TICKET. An
     omnibus. Lead. Rare.
302 HAVENS, HATTER, 202 Broadway. Lead.
303 HEWETT, Dr. J. G. BONE SETTER, 68 Prince St. Copper. Thick
     planchet.   . .
304 Same. Thin planchet.
305 HILL, E. Dealer in Coins, Medals, Curiosities, etc. 6 Bleecker St.
     1860. ℞ Head of Washington by Key. Silver.
306 Same. Brass.
307 Same. Copper.
308 Same. White metal.
309 Same obverse. ℞ Bust of Daniel Webster. Silver.
310 Same. Brass.
311 Same. Copper.
312 Same. White metal.
313 Same obverse. ℞ Bust of Edwin Forest. Silver.
314 Same. Brass.
315 Same. Copper.
316 Same. White metal.
317 Same obverse. ℞ The smoker. Silver.
318 Same. Brass.
319 Same. Copper.
320 Same. White metal.
321 Same obverse. ℞ Cupid. Silver.
322 Same. Brass.
323 Same. Copper.
324 Same. White metal.
325 Same obverse. ℞ Card of F. C. Key & Sons, Phila. Silver.
326 Same. Brass.
327 Same. Copper.
328 Same. White metal.
329 Same obverse. ℞ KEY in large letters. Silver.
330 Same. Brass.
331 Same. Copper.
332 Same. White metal.
333 Same obverse. ℞ Card of Woodgate & Co. N. Y. Silver.
334 Same. Brass.
335 Same. Copper.
336 Same. White metal.
337 Same obverse. ℞ VIRTUE, LIBERTY & INDEPENDENCE. Silver.
338 Same. Brass.

339 Same. Copper.

340 Same. White metal.

341 HOAG, T. CLOCKS & JEWELRY, 1373 B'way. ℞ Liberty head. White metal.

342 Same. ℞ Liberty bell. White metal.

343 Same. ℞ Continental soldier. White metal.

344 Same. Copper.

345 Same. ℞ Maryland arms. White metal.

346 Same. ℞ Independence Hall. Copper.

347 HOOKS, BENJAMIN, 276 BROOME ST. Bust of Franklin in fur cap. Silver. Extremely rare.

348 Same. Copper. Very rare.

349 Same. Silvered. Very rare.

350 Bust of Franklin as on preceding, small dog counterstamp. ℞ Blank. Copper. Rare.

351 HOOPS, H. W., CONFECTIONERY, 370 BOWERY. ℞ Liberty head. White metal.

352 Same. ℞ Liberty bell. White metal.

353 Same. Copper.

354 Same obverse. ℞ Continental soldier. White metal.

355 Same. ℞ Maryland arms. White metal.

356 HORTER, CHARLES D., 178 WILLIAM ST., DIE SINKER. ℞ Building (178 William St.) Silver. Very rare.

357 Same. Copper.

358 Same. White metal.

359 HOUGHTON, MERRELL & CO. Umbrellas & Parasols, 48 Cedar St. ℞ Umbrellas. Brass.

360 HUDNUTS MINERAL. ℞ Blank. Nickel.

361 HUYLER'S. 31 8th AVE. & 869 B'WAY. ℞ Liberty head. White metal.

362 Same. ℞ Liberty bell. White metal.

363 Same. ℞ Continental soldier. White metal.

364 Same. Copper. ℞ Maryland arms. White metal.

365 Same. ℞ Maryland arms. White metal.

366 Same ℞ Independence Hall. White metal.

367 Same. Copper.

368 IRVING, L. G. Anvil, arm with sledge. ℞ Card of P. S. Pease & Co. St. Louis. Brass. Excessively rare.

369 Same. Copper. Excessively rare.

370 JARVIS, GEORGE A. Wine and tea. Liberty head, star ornaments. Low 122. Copper.

371 Similar. Leaf ornaments. Low 123. Copper.

372 JEFFERSON INSURANCE CO. ℞ Lincoln by Bolen. White metal. 26m.

373 JENKINS, WILLIAM R. PRINTER & BOOKSELLER. ℞ Liberty head. White metal.

374 Same obverse. ℞ Liberty bell. White metal.

375 Same obverse. ℞ Continental soldier. White metal.

376 Same obverse. ℞ Maryland arms. White metal.

377   Same. ℞ Independence Hall. **Copper.**
378   JENNINGS WHEELER & CO. Clothing, 43 Chambers St. ℞ WHOLE-
         SALE CLOTHING WARE HOUSE. Brass. Milled edge.
— 379   Same. Brass. Plain edge.
— 380   Similar. Name of firm in large letters, two stars added. ℞ same at
         preceding. Brass. Plain edge . Rare.
381   Same obverse. ℞ Clasped hands, etc. Silver. Very rare.
382   Same. Copper.
383   Same. Brass. Milled edge.
384   Same. Brass. Plain edge.
— 385   Same. Brass, silvered. Reeded edge.
386   JENNINGS WHEELER & CO., 45-47 CHAMBERS ST. ℞ Map of
         North America. Copper.
387   Same. Brass. Milled edge.
388   Same. Brass. Plain edge.
389. Same obverse. ℞ Bust of Lincoln. Brass. Excessively rare.
390   Same obverse. ℞ Bust of Kossuth. Brass. Excessively rare.
391   Same. Copper. Excessively rare.
392   Same obverse. ℞ New York Crystal Palace. Brass. Excessively rare.
393   Same obverse. ℞ Card of N. C. Folger & Son, New Orleans. Brass.
         Map of North America. ℞ New York Crystal Palace. Brass. Ex-
         tremely rare.
394   Map of North America. ℞ Ship to r. ℞ of the card of Doremus, Suy-
         dam & Nixon. Brass. Extremely rare.
395   Same. ℞ Crystal Palace. Brass.
— 396   JOHNSON, PROF. SOAP & STARCH POLISH. Liberty **head.** ℞
         Eagle. Copper. Plain edge.
— 397   Same. Brass. Plain edge.
398   Same. German silver. Milled edge.
399   Obverse, reverse of the preceding. ℞ THERE IS NO DIFFICULTY TO
         HIM THAT WILLETH—Eagle. Brass. Extremely rare.
— 400   JOHNSON, PROF. Liberty head, 1852. ℞ Eagle. Brass. 21m.
401   JOHNSON, PROF. Bust of Kossuth three quarter facing to r. ℞
         same as preceding. Brass. 21m.
402   JOHNSON, PROF. CHEMICAL BLUEING. Liberty head. ℞ Same
         as obverse. Brass. 21m.
403   JONES, WILLIAM G. UNION COAL YARD. Copper. Very rare. ·
404   Same. Brass. Very rare.
405   J. E. Within ornamental border. ℞ Eagle. Copper. 20m. Scarce.
406   Same. Brass.
407   J. P. Within ornamental border. ℞ Similar to preceding. Copper.
         24m. Scarce.
408   Same. Brass. Scarce.
409   KAYSER, H. & M. & CO. FANCY GOODS. ℞ Eagle on rock. Brass.
         Rare.
410   Same. Lead. Rare.
411   KIPP BROWN & CO. CHELSEA LINE. ℞ TRANSFER TICKET. An
         omnibus. Lead. Rare.
412   KNAPP, J. C. MFG. CO. An oil lamp. ℞ ALL KINDS SHEET METAL
         WORK MADE TO ORDER. Brass shell. 24m. Very rare.

413 KRUGER, TH. RESTAURANT. ℞ BEER TICKET. 1876. An eagle. White metal. 22m.

414 LADIES RESTAURANT. 280 8th Ave. ℞ 1/. Brass.

415 Same. ℞ 3/. Brass.

416 LANE, DAVID H. RECORDER OF DEEDS. 1875. ℞ Lincoln by Bolen. White metal. 26m.

417 LAW H. BAKER 187 Canal St. Eagle. ℞ Sheaf of wheat. Copper.

418 LEASK, M. MOURNING & ILLUSION GOODS. White metal.

419 LEHR, F. NEEDLE THREADERS. Head of Lincoln. ℞ Eagle. Brass. 18m. Rare.

420 LEIGHTON, C. SHIRT MANUFACTURER, New York & New Orleans. Liberty seated. ℞ Head of Liberty with turban. Brass.

421 Same obverse. ℞ Eagle, legend begins and ends near tips of wings. Copper. Thick planchet.

422 Same. Brass.

423 Same. White metal.

424 Same obverse. ℞ Eagle's wings are more spread, the legend begins and ends near the top of each wing. Brass.

425 LEVERETT & THOMAS, Hardware, Cutlery, etc. Copper. Rare.

426 LEVICK, J. N. T. 1860 Pipes crossed over box of cigars. ℞ The smoker. Silver.

427 Same. Copper.

428 Same. Brass.

429 Same. White metal.

430 Same obverse. ℞ Head of Washington by Key. Copper.

431 Same. Brass.

432 Same. White metal.

433 Same obverse. ℞ Bust of Webster. Copper.

434 Same. Brass.

435 Same. White metal.

436 Same obverse. ℞ Bust of Edwin Forrest. Copper.

437 Same. Brass.

438 Same. White metal.

439 Same obverse. ℞ Cupid on seashore. Copper.

440 Same. Brass.

441 Same. White metal.

442 Same obverse. ℞ F. C. Key & Son's card. Copper.

443 Same. Brass.

444 Same. White metal.

445 Same obverse. ℞ KEY in large letters. Copper.

446 Same. Brass.

447 Same. White metal.

448 Same obverse . ℞ Card of Woodgate & Co. Silver.

449 Same. Copper.

450 Same. Brass.

451 Same. White metal.

452 Same obverse. ℞ VIRTUE, LIBERTY & INDEPENDENCE. Copper.

453 Same. Brass.

454 Same. White metal.

455 Same obverse. ℞ Card of E. Hill. Copper.
456 Same. Brass.
457 Same. White metal.
458 Same obverse. ℞ REPRESENTED BY J. N. T. LEVICK. Copper.
459 Same. Brass.
460 Same. White metal.
461 The smoker. ℞ Bust of Forrest. Copper.
462 Same. Brass.
463 Same. White metal.
464 LIEBERTZ, P. 113 BOWERY. 5 cent drink check. Brass.
465 LODER & CO., 83 CEDAR ST. Dry Goods. Eagle. ℞ Card with ad-
       dress repeated. Copper.
466 Same. Brass.
467 Same. Brass, silvered.
468 Same obverse. ℞ Map of North America. Silver. Very raer.
469 Same obverse. ℞ Eagle. DR. SELLECK, etc. Silver. Very rare.
470 Same. Copper. Rare.
471 Same obverse. ℞ Card of Doremus & Nixon. Silver. Very rare.
472 Same, White metal. Rare.
473 Same obverse. ℞ Vessel, reverse of Doremus & Nixon card. Brass.
       Rare.
474 LODER & CO., 130 BROADWAY. Eagle. ℞ Card with address, 83
       Cedar St., Copper.
475 Same. Brass. Reeded edge.
476 Same. Brass, silvered. Plain edge.
477 Same. ℞ Card of Doremus & Nixon. Brass. Rare.
478 Same. ℞ Importers & Jobbers &c. Copper.
479 LORILLARD, P. & CO. 1876. Monogram in wreath. ℞ 50. Border
       of stars. Copper. 37m.
480 Same. German silver.
481 Similar. ℞ 10. Brass. 25m.
482 Similar. ℞ 5. German silver. 20m.
483 Similar. ℞ 1. German silver. 17m.
484 Same. Brass.
485 LOVETT, 67 MAIDEN LANE. ENGRAVER & DIE SINKER. ℞ Ship
       at wharf, reverse die of Collins card. Brass. Very rare.
486 LOVETT, GEO. H. 131 FULTON ST . ℞ Cupid on seashore. 31m.
487 Same. Brass.
488 Same. White metal.
489 Same obverse. ℞ The antiquary. Copper.
490 Same. Brass.
491 Same. White metal.
492 Same obverse. ℞ John Bull and Brother Jonathan, reverse die of
       Atlantic Cable medal. 1858. Silver. Rare .
493 Same. Copper.
494 Same. Brass.
495 Same. White metal.
496 LOVETT, J. D., 1 COURTLAND ST. Seal press. ℞ WEDDING &
       VISITING CARDS, etc. Silver. Very rare.

497 Same. Copper.

498 Same. Brass.

499 Same. White metal.

500 NEW CONGRESS HALL (Saratoga) 1860. ℞ Same as preceding. Silver. Rare.

501 Same. Copper.

502 Same. Brass.

503 Obverse of the Lovett card. ℞ New Congress Hall. Brass.

504 LOVETT, R. MEDALLIST. ℞ Bust of Franklin. Silver. Rare.

505 Same. Copper.

506 Same. Brass.

507 LYON, E. 424 BROADWAY, INSECT POWDER, etc. Liberty head, E. LYON above. ℞ Eagle. Brass.

508 Similar. Six stars over head. Periods after BROADWAY and NEW. Brass.

509 Similar. Five smaller stars. Seven stars above head. Brass.

510 Similar type, reduced size. Brass. 20m.

511 LYON, E. Bust to r. ℞ Liberty seated. Brass.

512 MACY, R. H. & CO. 1876. Figure "7" on star. ℞ Boy and bear with soda syphon. Copper.

513 Similar. Figure "18·" Bronze.

514 MALE MORSONIC AMULET. ℞ Eagle. Copper. 34m. Rare.

515 MALCOLM & GAUL. Dry Goods, 62 Liberty St. Copper.

516 Same. Brass.

517 Same. Brass, silvered.

518 MANHATTAN WATCH CO., 234 Broadway. ℞ Watch dial. Copper.

519 Same. Brass.

520 Same. German silver.

521 MARSHALL & TOWNSEND, 7th Avenue Lines. ℞ TRANSFER TICKET. An omnibus Lead. Rare.

522 Similar. 6th & 7th Avenue Lines. Lead. Rare.

523 MATTHEWS, JOHN. SODA WATER APPARATUS. 1863. Liberty head in turban. Copper.

524 Same. Brass.

525 Similar obverse. ℞ Boy and bear with soda syphon. Copper.

526 Same. Bronze.

527 Head to right John Matthews, 1808-1870. ℞ as last, copper, silvered. Size 45. Scarce.

528 MAYCOCK, S. & CO. PENCILS, ETC. 35 City Hall Place. Eagle with 1837 below. ℞ Card. Copper, Low 126.

529 MAYCOCK, S. & CO. Crude Liberty head. ℞ Same as preceding. Copper. Low 125.

530 MEADE BROS. DAGUERREOTYPES. ℞ Eagle. Rare.

531 MERCHANTS EXCHANGE. View of old building. ℞ MILLIONS FOR DEFENCE. Within wreath—NOT ONE CENT FOR TRIBUTE. Dash below CENT and berry opposite second E in DEFENCE. Copper. Low 96. Extremely rare.

532 Similar. No dash under CENT. Copper. Common.

533 Similar. Dash under CENT but no berry opposite E. Copper. Common.

534   MERCHANTS EXCHANGE. View of new building. ℞ NEW YORK
      JOINT STOCK EXCHANGE, etc. Copper.

535   MERRITT, J. G., 12 Bowery, Clothing Emporium. Brass.

536   MERRITT & LANGLEY. MERRITT & LANGLEY'S DEY ST. HOUSE.
      ℞ DEY ST. DINING SALOON. German silver. No counterstamp.

537   Similar. Cs. on obverse and reverse. 2/3. German silver.

538   Similar. Cs. on obverse and reverse. 2/. German silver.

539   Similar. 1/3. German silver.

540   Similar. 3/3. German silver.

541   Similar. 3/6. German silver.

542   Similar. 3/9. German silver.

543   Similar. 4/. German silver.

544   Similar with 54 & 56 DEY ST. NEW YORK added in centre. ℞ Same
      as preceding with counterstamp on reverse only on all that follow.
      German silver.

545   Similar. /6. German silver.

546   Similar. /9. German silver.

547   Similar. 1/. German silver.

548   Similar. 1/3. German silver.

549   Similar. 1/6. German silver.

550   Similar. 1/9. German silver.

551   Similar. 2/. German silver.

552   Similar. 2/3. German silver.

553   Similar. 2/9. German silver.

554   Similar. 3/. German silver.

555   Similar. 3/3. German silver.

556   Similar. 3/6. German silver.

557   Similar. 4/. German silver.

558   MESCHUTT'S METROPOLITAN COFFEE ROOM 433. BD. WAY Coun-
      terstamp on Spanish 2 reales. Very rare.

559   Same on Irish halfpenny of 1805. Very rare.

560   Similar on thick white metal planchet, counterstamped "9." ℞ blank.

561   Similar, but large "O" with diagonal line. ℞ "1/-. " White metal.

562   Similar, but "3" counterstamp. Lead. All of this series scarce to rare.

563   METROPOLITAN CAVE. B'way & White St. ℞ 1/-. Brass.

564   Similar. ℞ 2/. Brass.

565   Similar. ℞ 3/. Brass.

566   Similar. ℞ 3/6. Brass.

567   Similar. R 5/. Brass.

568   Similar. ℞ 8/6. Brass.

569   Similar. ℞ 9/6. Brass.

570   Similar. ℞ 11/. Brass.

571   Similar. ℞ 11/6. Brass.

572   METROPOLITAN INSURANCE CO 1852. Sailing vessel to r. ℞ MA-
      RINE & FIRE, etc. CAPITAL $300,000. Silver. Rare.

573   Same. Copper.

574   Same. Brass. Rare.

575   Same obverse. ℞ 1865. CAPITAL $1,000,000. Copper.

576   Same. Brass.

577 Similar obverse. ℞ 1865. CAPITAL $300,000. Copper. Rare.

578 Same. Brass. Rare.

579 Similar obverse. ℞ 1866 DEALERS, etc. Copper. 31m.

580 Same. Brass. 31m.

581 MEYER, LEOPOLD Dr. Bust to l. ℞ LEOPOLD DE MEYER'S CON-CERT. Brass.

582 MILLER. USE MILLER'S HAIR INVIGORATOR 295 BOWERY, N. Y. This counterstamp or a similar one is found on many coins.

583 MODEL ARTIST EXHIBITION. ADMIT TO THE MODEL ARTIST'S 127 GRAND ST. NEAR B'WAY. Struck on a Spanish 2 reales. Rare.

584 Same. Struck in quarter dollar. Dated 1807. Rare.

585 MOFFET, JAMES G. BRASS FOUNDER, 121 Prince St. Eagle with scroll above. Flower ornaments on reverse. Copper.

586 Similar. Motto on scroll reads PLUBIBUS. No flower ornaments on reverse. Copper.

587 MOSS' HOTEL. Cor. Bowery & Bayard. ℞ Blank. Copper.

588 Same. Brass.

589 Same. ℞ 6d. Brass.

590 Same. ℞ 1/. Brass.

591 Same. ℞ 1/. Brass.

592 Same. ℞ 1/3. Brass.

593 Same. ℞ 1/6. Brass.

594 Same. ℞ 1/9. Brass.

595 Same. ℞ 2/. Brass.

596 Same. ℞ 2/3. Brass.

597 Same. ℞ 2/6. Brass.

598 Same. ℞ 2/9. Brass.

599 Same. ℞ 3/. Brass.

600 Same. ℞ 3/3. Brass.

601 Same. ℞ 3/6. Brass

602 Same. ℞ 3/9. Brass.

603 Same. ℞ 4/. Brass.

604 Same. ℞ Sweeny's Hotel. Copper.

605 Same. Brass.

606 Same. ℞ Smithsonian House. Copper.

607 Same. Brass.

608 Same. ℞ A. D. Thompson. Copper.

609 Same. Brass.

610 MOTTS. JEWELERS, CLOCKS AND WATCHES. 1789. A tall clock. ℞ Eagle. Copper. Thick planchet.

611 Same. Thin planchet.

612 Same. Engrailed edge.

613 Same. Edge lettered PAYABLE AT LIVERPOOL, LONDON OR BRISTOL.

NOTE.—A majority of the specimens found are struck from broken dies

614 MOTT, WM. H., HARDWARE, CUTLERY, ETC. OLD SLIP & WATER ST. Brass.

615 Similar. OLD SHIP & WAER ST. Brass.

616 MULLEN, WM. J., GOLD DIAL MFG. Head to l. ℞ Infants making dials. Copper. 33m.

617 MYERS, JIM. Great American Circus. Eagle. ℞ Uninscribed three circles. Brass. Very rare.

618 NATIONAL JOCKEY CLUB. Jockey on horse to r. Brass. 25m. Rare.

619 NEW YORK & HARLEM RAILROAD. ℞ An old railroad coach. By Bale and Smith. Octagonal. Copper. 18m. Rare.

620 Same. German silver. Rare.

621 Same. Lead. Rare.

622 Same. Small ornament incuse in field of obverse. German silver. Rare.

623 Same. Small dog, incuse in field of obverse. German silver. Rare.

624 NEW YORK S. D. & CO. Silver. Square. 22m. (Cogan catalogue Sept. 1878).

625 ONE HUNDRED STREET. 100 STREET. ℞ Same as obverse. Copper.

626 PARMELE, EDWIN. Old man with glass of wine. ℞ BOWLING SALOON KEPT BY EDWIN PARMELE 340 PEARL ST. Brass. 18m. Extremely rare.

627 PARISIAN VARIETIES. 16 ST. & B'WAY. N. Y. Incuse on 1875 Half Dollar. (Betts sale No. 19) Very rare.

628 PARMELEE, WEBSTER & CO. 155 Jane St. Bust of Grant to r. ℞ 10 PURE ALUMINUM. Silver. Rare.

629 Same. Copper.

630 Same. Brass.

631 Same. White metal.

632 PEALE'S MUSEUM AND GALLERY OF THE FINE ARTS 1825. Mailed busts to l. ℞ ADMIT THE BEARER, etc. Copper. 34m.

633 Same. White metal. Rare.

634 PHALON. 1837. HAIR CUTTING. ℞ Scissors and comb. Copper. Low 127.

635 PHELAN, GEO. E., BILLIARDS. ℞ Liberty head. White metal.

636 Same. ℞ Liberty bell. White metal.

637 Same ℞ Continental soldier. White metal.

638 Same. Copper.

639 Same. ℞ Maryland arms. White metal.

640 PIMMEL, W., SEWING MACHINE AGENT. ℞ Liberty head. White metal.

641 Same. ℞ Liberty bell. White metal.

642 Same. ℞ Continental solder. White metal.

643 Same. ℞ Maryland arms. White metal.

644 PRENTICE, F., MINING, 26 Pine St. View of mine and buildings. Silver. 31m.

645 PRESCOTT'S, 11 Wall St. Soda Water. ℞ Eagle. German silver. 17m. Scarce.

646 PRUDENS, 66 W. 13 St. Pictures and Fireworks. ℞ Liberty head. White metal.

647   Same. ℞ Liberty bell. White metal.

648   Same. ℞ Continental soldier. White metal.

649   Same. ℞ Maryland arms. White metal.

650   Same. ℞ Independence Hall. Copper.

651   RAHM, LOUIS, COPPERSMITH, 178 William St. ℞ View of building occupied by Horter & Rahm. Silver. Rare.

652   Same. Copper.

653   Same. White metal.

654   RATHBONE & FITCH, 1825, CASTLE GARDEN. View of Castle Garden. ℞ JONATHAN RATHBONE & FRANCIS B. FITCH, PROPRIETORS, 1825. Flying eagle with scroll. 48x25m. Excessively rare.

655   REDFIELD & RICE, NEW YORK with star between two flowers above and below, small eagle in exergue. ℞ Blank. Lead. 23m. Very rare.

656   RICHARDSON, STEPHEN, Mf'g of Jewelry. Bust to l. ℞ Eagle. Brass. 23m.

657   RICHARDSON, WM. H., 229 Broadway. Umbrellas. Brass. 24m.

658   Similar but 418 Market St. Philada. added on obverse. Brass.

659   RIKER, ABRAHAM., Boots and Shoes, 131 Division St, ℞ MILLIONS FOR DEFENCE etc. Wreath has five berries inside and three outside. Copper. Low 153.

660   Similar. Wreath has six berries inside and two outside. Copper. Low 154.

661   RIKER, J. L. & D. J. 1852. Mfg. of Knife & Scissors Sharpeners. Brass. 21m.

662   Same obverse. ℞ Eagle. Brass.

663   RISLEY & McCULLUM'S HIPPODROME. Circus rider on two horses to r. ℞ TROISIEME. Brass. Rare.

664   Same. Copper.

665   Same. Silvered.

666   ROBBINS, ROYCE & HARD, Wholesale Dealers in Dry Goods, 70 Reade St., New York. ℞ Bust of Washington. Silver. (Seven struck.)

680   Same.   Nickel.   250 struck.

681   Bust of Lincoln.   WIDEAWAKES.   Silver.   21 struck.

682   Same.   Copper.   35 struck.

683   Same.   Brass.   35 struck.

684   Same.   Nickel.   35 struck.

685   Same.   Block tin.   1500 struck.

686   ROBBINS, ROYCE & HARD, 70 READE ST.   ℞ Lincoln.   Silver.

687   Same.   Copper.

688   Same.   Brass.

689   Same.   Nickel.

690   Same.   White metal.

691   ROBBINS, ROYCE & HARD, 70 READE & 112 DUANE ST.   ℞ Lincoln.   Silver.

692   Same.   Copper.

693   Same.   Brass.

694   Same.   Nickel.

695   Same.   White metal.

696   Same obverse as 686.   70 Reade St.   ℞ Wideawakes.   Silver.

697   Same.   Copper.

698   Same.   Brass.

699   Same.   Nickel.

700   Same.   White metal.

701   Same obverse as 691.   70 Reade & 112 Duane St.   ℞ Wideawakes.   Silver.

702   Same.   Copper.

703   Same.   Brass.

704   Same.   Nickel.

705   Same.   White metal.

706   Ob. Lincoln.   ℞ Wideawakes.   Silver.

707   Same.   Copper.

708   Same.   Brass.

709   Same.   Nickel.

710   Same.   White metal.

711   Same obverse as 686.   70 Reade St.   ℞ same as obverse of 70 Reade & 112 Duane St.   Silver.

712   Same.   Copper.

713   Same.   Brass.

714   Same.   Nickel.

715   Same.   White metal.

716   Same obverse as 686.   70 Reade St.   ℞ Washington.   Silver.

717   Same.   Copper.

718   Same.   Brass.

719   Same.   Nickel.

720   Same.   White metal.

721   Same obverse as 691.   70 Reade & 112 Duane St.   ℞ Washington.   Silver.

722   Same.   Copper.

723   Same.   Brass.

724   Same.   Nickel.

725 Same. White metal.

726 ROBINSON, R. & W. Military Naval, Sporting & Plain Flat Buttons. Copper. (Low 103.)

727 Same. ℞ similar to last, but date, "1836" further from the word "BUTTONS." Copper. (Low 104.)

728 Same, but hyphen between "NEW" and "YORK" in the exergue. ℞ same as Low 103. Copper. (Low 105.) Scarce.

— 729 ROBINSON, JONES & CO. Copper. (Low 75.)

— 730 Similar to last, but from different die. "1" in date is small and slightly slanting. Copper. (Low 76.)

731 ROOT & CO., DAGUERROTYPE GALLERY. ℞ FIRST PREMIUM AWARDED TO ROOT & CO. FOR BEST DAGUERROTYPES. Copper.

732 Same. Brass. Reeded edge.

733 Obverse is the reverse of the last. ℞ Eagle. THERE IS NO DIFFICULTY TO HIM THAT WILLETH. Copper.

734 Same. Brass.

735 ROWELL, GEO. P., & CO., NEWSPAPER ADVERTISING, 41 PARK ROW, NEW YORK. ℞ Liberty Bell. Copper.

736 Same. White metal.

737 Same. ℞ Liberty head. White metal.

738 Same. ℞ Continental soldier. White metal.

739 Same. Maryland coat of arms. White metal.

740 Same. ℞ Public Buildings, Philadelphia. White metal.

741 Same. ℞ Independence Hall. Copper.

742 ROYAL PREVENTIVE. ℞ Eagle in circle of stars. Copper. Very rare.

743 Same. Brass. Very rare.

744 Same. Tin. Very rare.

— 745 RUGGLES, ROBERT B., GOLD BEATER. Copper.

— 746 Similar obverse, with "BALE N. Y." in small letters. Copper.

747 RUSSELL, R. E., "I. O. U. 12½c." Feuchtwanger metal. (Low 128.) Very rare.

748 SACHEM OYSTER SALOON, 273 BOWERY. Struck over Spanish 2 reales. Extremely rare.

749 SAGE, A. B. & CO., DEALER IN COINS, MEDALS & TOKENS, &c. 1860. ℞ CITY HALL, WALL ST. N. Y. View of building. Silver.

750 Same. Copper.

751 Same. Brass.

752 Same. White metal.

753 Same obverse as last. ℞ SIR HENRY CLINTON'S HOUSE. Silver.

754 Same. Copper.

755 Same. Brass.

756 Same. White metal.

757 SAGE, A. B., & CO. CIRCULATION LIBRARY, 24 DIVISION ST., N. Y. ℞ Bust of Washington, "PATER PATRIAE." Silver.

758 Same. Copper.

759 Same. Brass.

760 Same. White metal.
761 SAGE, A. B., & CO. GOOD FOR ONE CHANCE IN RAFFLE FOR
     NUMISMATIC BOOKS, NOV. 1859. ℞ Same as last. Silver.
762 Same. Copper.
763 Same. Brass.
764 Same. White metal.
765 Ob. "RAFFLE." ℞ "CIRCULATING LIBRARY." Brass.
766 SAGE, A. B., & CO. Size 10. Copper.
767 Same. Brass.
768 Same. White metal.
769 SANS SOUCI. Lead. Rare.
770 SAMPSON, H. G., DEALER IN RARE AMERICAN & FOREIGN COINS,
     &c. 91 Bushwick Ave., Brooklyn. ℞ Declaration of Independence.
     Size 45m. Silver.
771 Same. Copper.
772 Same. Brass.
773 Same. White metal.
774 Same obverse. ℞ Bust of Washington. Silver.
775 Same. Copper.
776 Same. Brass.
777 Same. Brass.
778 Same. White metal.
779 SCHMIDT, EDWARD. RESTAURANT, 194 FULTON ST., N. Y.
     Figure "2" counterstamped in centre. ℞ Eagle. Brass. 30m.
780 Same, but counterstamped "1." Brass.
781 Same, but counterstamped "50." Brass.
782 SCHOONMAKER, W. H., 181 BROADWAY, N. Y., GUNS, PISTOLS,
     &c. ℞ MILITARY GOODS, SILVER PLATED BRITANNIA AND
     FANCY ARTICLES. Brass . Size 26m.
783 Same. German silver. Extremely rare.
784 Same. ℞ Bust of Jackson. Brass. Very rare.
785 Same. ℞ Bust of George IV. of England. Brass. Very rare.
786 SCOTT, J. W., & CO., 146 FULTON ST., N. Y. ℞ Liberty bell. Cop-
     per.
787 Same. Brass.
788 Same. White metal.
789 Same. ℞ Arms of Maryland. Copper.
790 Same. Brass.
791 Same. White metal.
792 Same. ℞ Independence Hall. Copper.
793 Same. Brass.
794 Same. White metal.
795 Same. ℞ Continental soldier. Brass.
796 Same. White metal.
797 Same. Copper.
798 Same. ℞ Carpenters' Hall. Brass.
799 Same. ℞ Liberty Head. Copper.
800 Same. Brass.
801 Same. White metal.

— 802 SCOVILL MANUFACTURING CO., 57 MAIDEN LANE, N. Y. MANU-
FACTURERS OF ROLL BRASS, &c. Copper.

— 803-804 Same. Brass. Reeded edge.

— 805 SCOVILLS DAGUERROTYPE MATERIALS, 101 WILLIAM ST., NEW
YORK. Brass.

806 SEA ISLAND SHIRTS, 57 LIBERTY STREET, NEW YORK. Brass.
size 15m. Very rare.

807 SEITZ BROS. ONE BIER. ℞ Female head. (Similar in style to Ehret
and Eichler cards. Brass. 23m. Plain edge. Rare.

— 808 SMITHS CLOCK ESTABLISHMENT NO 7½ BOWERY NEW YORK
1837. ℞ clock dial. The hour hand touches right part of "X."
Copper. (Low 133.)

809 Similar to last. Hour hand points to centre of "X." Copper. (Low
134.)

— 810 Obverse similar to Low 133. Word "ESTABLISHMENT" is curved.
Copper. (Low 135.)

— 811 Similar to last, but floral ornaments at either side. ℞ the minute hand
points to the third mark following "II." The "V" in "VIII" points
to the centre of "M" in "MONEY." Copper. (Low 136.)

812 Similar to last, but the floral ornaments are much larger. Copper.
(Low 138.)

812a Same. Struck on a planchet gilded before striking. Very rare.

813 SMITH, JAS. S., & CO., MILITARY GOODS, 15 DUTCH ST., N. YORK.
Military cap in centre of field. The inscription "15 DUTCH ST. N.
YORK" in circle. Copper.

814 Same. Brass.

815 Same.

816 Same obverse as last. ℞ similar to last, but the inscription "No. 15
DUTCH ST. N. YORK" in three horizontal lines. Brass. Very rare.

817 SMITH F. B., & HARTMANN, MEDAL & GENERAL DIE-SINKERS &
ENGRAVERS. 122 FULTON ST. COR. NASSAU, NEW YORK.
1860. Indian head in field of obverse. Copper. Reeded edge.

— 818 Same. Brass. Reeded edge.

819 Same. White metal. Reeded edge.

820 Same obverse of Indian head as foregoing. ℞ Flora Temple. Brass.

821 SMITH & SEWARD, MANUFACTURERS OF MEDALS COINS BADGES
92 FULTON 130 & 132 William Sts., NEW YORK. ℞ Lion ram-
pant. Aluminum. 31½m. Plain edge.

822 Same. ℞ a running horse. White metal. 31½m. Plain edge.

823 SMITHSONIAN HOUSE, 606 BROADWAY, ℞ blank. Copper.

824 Same. Brass.

825 Same. ℞ 3/. Brass.

826 Same. ℞ 10/6. Brass.

827 SQUIRE & MERRITT, SHIP CHANDLERS, &c, ℞ DEALERS IN
ANCHORS, OILS, &c. Copper. Bread milling.

828 Same as foregoing. Figures "175" incused above "SOUTH St." Silver.
Very rare.

829 Same. Copper.

830 Same with "1836" incused. Copper.

831 Similar to foregoing; but inscriptions surrounded by circles of pellets or dots. No milling or reeding on the edge. Copper.

832 SQUIRE, LEWIS L., & SONS, SHIP CHANDLERS & ROPE MAKERS, 283 FRONT ST., NEW YORK. ℞ similar wording to foregoing, but entirely different die. Silver. Very rare.

833 Same. Copper. Thick planchet.

834 Same. Copper. Thin planchet.

835 Same. Brass.

836 Same. White metal. (The latter specimen on very thick planchet.)

837 Same. ℞ VIRTUE LIBERTY & INDEPENDENCE. Lead. Unique.

838 STINER TEA COMPANY, N. Y. & CHINA. M. H. MOSES & CO. PROPS. ℞ Independence Hall. 24m. White metal.

839 STINER, JOS,, & CO., IMPORTERS OF TEAS & COFFEES, NEW YORK. ℞ ESTABLISHED 1840. "¼ *" in field. Brass.

840 Similar to last. ℞ "½ * " in field. Brass.

841 STRASSBURGER & NUHN, CORNER MAIDEN LANE & WILLIAM STREET. View of New York City Hall. ℞ Eagle, IN UNITATE FORTITUDO. Brass. 14½ m.

842 Same as last. ℞ Bust of Washington. Inscription, "GENERAL WASH-INGTON." Large letters. Brass. 14½ m.

843 Ob. of reverse of first variety. ℞ of reverse of second variety, Washington. Brass. 14½ m.

844 Similar to last, but from different and reduced dies. Brass. 12½ m.

845 STRASSBURGER & NUHN IMPORTERS 65 MAIDEN LANE, NEW YORK. ℞ Eagle. NO NORTH. NO SOUTH. ONE FLAG. ONE UNION. Brass. 14½ m.

846 STRASSBURGER & NUHN. View of Capitol at Washington. ℞ Washington. Small letters. Brass. 14½ m.

847 STRASSBURGER & NUHN. Size and design of U. S. double eagle. Brass.

848 SUYDAM & BOYD, IMPORTERS & DEALERS IN DRY GOODS, 157 PEARL ST. ℞ "Hy. SUYDAM Wm. BOYD, CLOTHS, CASIMERES, &c. Brass.

849 SUYDAM & BOYD, 187 PEARL ST. ℞ same as last. Brass.

850 SWEENY'S HOTEL, CORNER OF CHATHAM & DUANE STS, NEW YORK. Vertical line in centre. ℞ D. SWEENY & SON. Vertical line in centre. German silver.

851 Same. "1/ " in field. German silver.

852 Same. "1/3" in field. German silver.

853 Same. "2/-" in field. German silver.

854 Same. 2/6" in field. German silver.

855 Same. "2/6" in field. German silver.

855a Same. "3/" in field. German silver.

856 SWEENEY'S HOTEL, 64 CHATHAM ST. N. Y. ℞ SWEENEY'S DIN-ING SALOON, 64 CHATHAM ST., N. Y. German silver.

857 Same. but "13" in field. German silver.

858 Same. "50" in field. German silver.

859 Same. "87" in field. German silver.

860 Same. "94" in field. German silver.

861 SWEENY'S HOTEL. ℞ blank. Copper.

862 Same. ℞ "15" in field. Brass.

863 Same. ℞ "SMITHSONIAN" Copper.

864 Same. . Brass.

865 Same. ℞ "A. D. THOMPSON." Brass.

865 SWEET, EZRA B., 200 CANAL STREET, NEW YORK, STOVE &
 KITCHEN FURNITURE WAREHOUSE, &c. Liberty head, dated
 1837. Copper. Small planchet. (Low 140.)

866 Similar to foregoing. Large planchet. Copper. (Low 141.)

867 SWIFT & FARGO AMERICAN HOTEL, 135 FULTON ST. ℞ diagonal
 line. Brass.

868 Same. ℞ "6d" Brass.

869 Same. ℞ "2/ " Brass.

870 Same. ℞ "1/6" Brass.

871 Same. ℞ "2/6" Brass.

872 Same. ℞ "5/ " Brass.

873 Same. ℞ "5/6" Brass.

874 Same. ℞ "7/-" Brass.

875 Same. ℞ "9/6" Brass.

876 Same. ℞ "13/ " Brass.

877 TALBOT, ALLUM & LEE. 1794. Edge, PAYABLE AT THE STORE
 OF. Copper.

878 Same. . Plain edge. Large "&." Copper.

— 879 Similar to last, but "&" much smaller. Edge, PAYABLE AT THE
 STORE OF, but differently made edge. Copper.

880 Similar design to foregoing, but words "NEW YORK" omitted. Cop-
 .per. V. Rare.

— 881 TALBOT, ALLUM & LEE. 1795. Edge, WE PROMISE TO PAY THE
 BEARER ONE CENT. Copper.

882 Same as last. Plain edge.

883 Same. ℞ Naked boy. BIRMINGHAM HALFPENNY. 1793. Conder
 163—20 Edge. PAYABLE IN LONDON. Copper.

884 Same. ℞ a stork, "PROMISSORY HALFPENNY." 1793. Conder
 42—14 Edge, "PAYABLE IN LONDON." Copper.

—— 885 Same as last. Edge, "PAYABLE AT THE WAREHOUSE LIVER-
 POOL." Copper.

— 886 TALBOT, ALLUM & LEE. 1794. ℞ Bust of "JOHN HOWARD, F. R.
 S., PHILANTHROPIST." Condor 224—123. Edge, "PAYABLE IN
 LONDON." Copper. V. Rare.

887 Same as last. ℞ ADMIRAL EARL HOWE. Conder 204—26. Copper. V. Rare.

888 Same as last. ℞ BLOFIELD CAVALRY. Conder 118—6. Copper.
 V. Rare.

· 889 TAYLOR, J. M. Broker, Chatham St., cor. James, N. Y., counterstamped
 on quarter dollar of 1853. Very rare.

890 TAYLOR & SON, No. 45 CEDAR ST., NEW YORK, IMPORTERS AND
 AGENTS FOR SCOVILLE GILT WILLISTONS LASTING HORN
 BONE AND OTHER KINDS OF BUTTONS. Brass.

891 TAYLOR & RICHARDS. ℞ same as last. Brass.

892 THE THEATRE AT NEW YORK. View of theatre. ℞ MAY COM-
 MERCE FLOURISH. Edge lettered. I Promise to Pay the Bearer
 on demand One Penny. Copper. Very rare.

893   Same. Copper. Plain edge. Very rare.

894   THIRD AVENUE RAILROAD. Omnibus. ℞ "HARLEM." Lead. Rare.

895   Same. ℞ "YORKVILLE." Lead. Rare.

896   Same. Street car. ℞ "HARLEM." Lead. Rare.

897   Same. Street car. ℞ "YORKVILLE." Lead. Rare.

898   THOMAS, R. F., JEWELER, 247 GRAND ST. Brass.

899   THOMPSON, A. D. ℞ blank. Copper.

900   Same. Brass.

901   Same. ℞ "1/6." Copper.

902   Same. Brass.

903   Same. ℞ "2/ " Copper.

904   Same. Brass.

905   Same. ℞ "2/6 " Copper.

906   Same. Brass.

907   Same. ℞ SWEENY'S HOTEL. Copper.

908   Same. Brass.

909   Same. ℞ SMITHSONIAN HOUSE. Copper.

910   Same. Brass.

911   THOMPSON, S. H. ℞ blank. Brass. 25m. Rare.

912   Same. ℞ "2/6." Brass. 25m.

913   T. P. D. 50. ℞ eagle, surrounded by thirteen stars. Brass. 28m.

914   T. P. D. 25   10m.

915   TRAPHAGEN, HUNTER & CO. Clothers. ℞ Liberty head. White metal.

916   Same. ℞ Independence Hall. Copper.

917   Same. ℞ Carpenters 8 Hall. White metal.

918   Same. ℞ Continental soldier. Copper.

919   TREDWELL, S. L., 228 PEARL ST. CHINA, GLASS & EARTHEN-WARE. ℞ same as obverse. Copper. 29m. Very rare.

920   TREDWELL, KISSAM & CO. HARDWARE, CUTLERY, &c. ℞ NEW YORK GRAND CANAL. Eagle. Brass.

921   Same, but "PEARL ST." in small letters after "CO." ℞ same as last. Brass.

922   TRESTED, RICHARD, Die Sinker & Stamper. ℞ shield. Brass. 14½m. Very rare.

923   TRESTED, RICHARD. Obverse the same as the reverse of foregoing. ℞ "SIX CENTS." Brass. 14½m. Very rare.

924   TRESTED, RICHARD, Engraver, Die Sinker & Stamper. ℞ eagle. Brass. 18m. Very rare.

925   TRESTED. Similar design to foregoing, but entirely different die. "R." for Richard omitted. ℞ same as foregoing. Struck over United States cent. Unique.

926   TYSON & CO. TELEGRAPH LINE. (Period after "TYSON." ℞ Omnibus. "TRANSFER TICKET." Brass.

927   TYSON & CO. TELEGRAPH LINE. (No period) X same as last. Brass.

938   UPSONS CAPITOL, 349 BROADWAY, COR. LEONARD. ℞ "6d." Brass.

929   Same. "3/-." Brass.

936   WARNER, 104 BARCLAY ST. ℞ ornamental with star in centre. No hyphen between "NEW" and "YORK." White metal. Extremely rare.

937   Similar to foregoing. Hyphen between "NEW" and "LORK." Silver. Rare.

938   Same. Copper. Rare.

939   Same. Brass. Rare.

940   Same. White metal. Rare.

941   WATERS, HORACE, & SONS, 481 BROADWAY, NEW YORK. PIANOS & ORGANS. ℞ view of organ and inscription. Small cross surmounts organ. White metal.

942   Same. ℞ similar, but no cross over organ, which is of different style. White metal.

943   CONGRESS HALL HOTEL, 142 BROADWAY, NEW YORK . Copper.

944   Same. Brass.

945   WELCH, URIAH, ST. NICHOLAS, NEW YORK. Rooster. Copper.

946   WELLENKAMP, HUGO, 53 BOWERY, N. Y. COLOSSEUM. Incused. Brass. Plain reverse.

947   Same, inscription, but different die. Brass.

948   WEST'S, H. B., TRAINED DOGS. Man driving dogs, "TRAY & TROY." ℞ New York Crystal Palace. Copper. Plain edge.

949   Same. Brass. Reeded edge.

950   Same. ℞ Obverse of Brown, Curtis & Vance Louisville card. Brass.

951   Same. View of "The Rail Splitter of the West." Brass. V. rare.

952   Same. ℞ obverse of N. C. Folger card. Brass.

953   WILLIAMS, Rd., UNION HALL. Copper. 19½ m. Very rare.

954   WILLIS & BROTHERS, CHINA, &c. Tin. Very rare.

955   WISE, A., DRY GOODS. Copper.

956   WOLFE'S SCHIEDAM SCHNAPPS. White metal.

957   WOLFE C. & I. D. ℞ NEW YORK GRAND CANAL. 1823. Brass.

958   WOLFE, CLARK & SPIES. Bust of Washington. ℞ Bust of Jackson in oval frame. Word "JACKSON" above. Brass. Very rare.

959   WOLFE, SPIES & CLARK. Bust of Washington. ℞ Bust of Jackson in octagonal frame, with "PRESIDENT" above. Brass. Very rare.

960   Same. Copper. Very rare.

961   Same. ℞ NEW YORK GRAND CANAL. 1823. Brass. Very rare.

962   Same. ℞ Bust of Jackson in oval frame, with inscription "CUTLERY, PLATED WARE, GUNS, &c." Brass. Very rare.

963 Same. ℞ Bust of George IV. of England. Brass. Very rare.
964 WOOD'S MINSTRELS. 1857. Silver. 25m.
965 Same. Copper. Very rare.
966 WOODCOCK, WM. P., BUTCHER. ℞ Woodcock. Copper. 32m.
967 Same. Brass.
968 Same. White metal.
969 WOODGATE & CO., IMPORTERS OF BRANDIES, WINES, &c. ℞
   REPRESENT. BY J. N. T. LEVICK, Copper.
970 Same. Brass.
971 Same. White metal.
972 Same. ℞ Bust of Washington. PATRIAE PATER. 1782. Copper.
973 Same. Brass.
974 Same. White metal.
975 Same. ℞ Bust of Webster. Copper.
976 Same. Brass.
977 Same. White metal.
978 Same. ℞ Bust of Forrest. Copper.
979 Same. Brass.
980 Same. White metal.
981 Same. Bust of a man smoking a cigar. "NO PLEASURE CAN EX-
   CEED," &c. Copper.
982 Same. Brass.
983 Same. White metal.
984 Same. ℞ Cupid. Copper.
985 Same. Brass.
986 Same. White metal.
987 Same. ℞ "F. C. KEY & SONS, 123 ARCH ST., PHILADA." Copper.
988 Same. Brass.
989 Same. White metal.
990 Same. ℞ large letters "K E Y," 329 Arch St., Phila. Copper.
991 Same. Brass.
992 Same. White metal.
993 Same. ℞ Two crossed pipes above cigar box. "LEVICK, 904 BROAD-
   WAY, NEW YORK. 1860." Copper.
994 Same. Brass.
995 Same. White metal.
996 Same. ℞ "VIRTUE, LIBERTY & INDEPENDENCE." Silver.
997 Same. Copper.
998 Same. Brass.
999 Same. White metal.
1000 WRIGHT & BALE. Bust of Franklin. Brass. 30m. Extremely rare.
1001 Same. Copper.
1002 WRIGHT & BALE. Bust of Washington. Copper. 15m. Thick
   planchet.
1003 Same. Copper. Thin planchet.
1004 WYMAN, WIZARD & VENTRILOQUIST. Struck over Spanish 2 reales.
1005 YOUNG & WARD, 6th AVENUE LINES. ℞ Omnibus. "TRANSFER
   TICKET." White metal. Rare.
1006 Y. & Co. 1 GLASS. ℞ Liberty head. Brass. Rare.

1017 HENDERSON & LOSSING, CLOCK AND WATCH MAKERS. **Copper.** 14m. V. Rare.

ROCHESTER.

—1018 OLCOTT BROTHERS, LOCOMOTIVE RR LAMP MANUFACTURERS. In field two kinds of locomotive headlights. Brass. 27m.

1019 OLCOTT & BROTHER, MANFTRS OF LOCOMOTIVE HEADLIGHTS ROCHESTER, N. Y. ℞ large locomotive headlight in plain field. Brass.

1020 Obverse, reverse of last. ℞ MOST EXTENSIVE IN THE UNITED STATES, etc. Eagle. White metal. ℞ of card of Sleeper & Fenner, Phila.

1021 Same. Brass, silvered.

—1022 STARR, FREDERICK, Musical instruments. Brass. 22m.

RENSSELAER.

1023 BRUNK, FRANK M. 5c ℞ Plain Brass. V. Rare.

SARATOGA.

—1024 BROWN, W. R. Congress Hall. Liberty head. Brass . 29m.

1025 CONGRESS HALL. Long serratures around legend. ℞ blank. **Copper.** 20m.

SYRACUSE.

1026 JUDSON, HIRAM, WATCH MAKER & SILVER SMITH. **Copper.** Thin planchet. 28m.

1027 Same. Copper. Thick planchet.

—1028 YATES, A. C., CLOTHING EMPORIUM. Brass. Reeded edge.

1029 Same. Copper. Plain edge.

1030 Same obverse. ℞ THE RAIL SPLITTER OF THE WEST. Brass. Rare.

1031 Same obverse. ℞ NEW YORK CRYSTAL PALACE. 1853. Copper.

1032 Same. Brass.

1033 Same obverse. ℞ DOREMUS & NIXON, with ship in field, DRY GOODS, & UPHOLSTERY FOR SHIPS & STEAMERS. Copper.

1034 Same. Brass.

TROY.

1035 BOUTWELL, O & P. NO 7 GRAND DIVISION ST., TROY, N. Y. 1835. ℞ BAKERS & CONFECTIONERS. Sheaf of wheat in centre. Copper. (Low 87.) Very rare.

1036 Same. Struck over Spanish 4 reales. Unique. (Low 174.)

1037 BUCKLIN'S BOOK KEEPING. TROY. Latter word inclosed in wreath. ℞ BUCKLIN'S INTEREST TABLES. In circle of stars the date "1835," below, in tiny letters, "TRUE ALB." Copper. (Low 93.)

1038 Same obverse. ℞ similar to last, but only "T * " below date. Copper. (Low 92.)

1039 BUCKLIN'S BOOK KEEPING SIMPLIFIED, &c. ℞ SHOWS THE INTEREST AT A GLANCE, &c. Copper. (Low 77.) Very rare.

1040 BUCKLIN'S BOOK KEEPING, WEST TROY, latter two words in centre, inclosed by wreath. ℞ Female head to left surrounded by fourteen stars. Copper. (Low 145.)

1041 Obverse same as reverse of Low 92—"T *" below date. ℞ Female head to right, with coronet inscribed "TROY." Fourteen stars around border, but none below the head. Copper. (Low 88.)

1042 Same obverse. ℞ Female head to right, ill-shaped and poorly executed with "TROY" on coronet, surrounded by fourteen stars, evenly spaced, with two below the head. Copper. (Low 89.)

1043 Same obverse. ℞ Female head to left, without stars, coronet inscribed "TROY." Copper. (Low 90.)

1044 Same obverse. ℞ Female head to right, similar to Low 89, but more shapely. Thirteen stars around border, quite distant from edge, but none directly below the bust. Copper. (Low 91.)

1045 CARPENTER & MOSHER, RIVER ST. In centre of field, inclosed by a wreath the words, "DRY GOODS" in two lines. Copper. (Low 146.) Very rare.

1046 Obverse same as last, but the number "310" below the word "GOODS." Copper. (Low 147.) Very rare.

1047 HASKINS, W. P., 435 RIVER ST., TROY, N. Y. 1834. ℞ WOODWORTH'S PATENT. A wood planing machine in field. Copper. (Low 80.)

1048 Same obverse. ℞ Lafayette. Copper. (Low 79.)

1049 PECK, J. & C. ℞ Tin machine and inscription. Copper.

1050 Same obverse. ℞ eagle. Copper.

1051 PERCY, E. L., TRUNKS, BAGS, ETC. Brass.

1052 STARBUCK & SON, PLOUGHS, PLOUGH CASTINGS, &c., ℞ MACHINE SHOP, TURNING & BORING, &c. Screw and belt and nut in field. Copper.

stars around border, same as reverse of Low 88. Copper. (Low 156.)

1054 Obverse same as last. R Female head to right, fourteen stars around border, evenly spaced, two being below head. Copper. (Low 157.) Very rare.

UTICA.

1055 Same. Silvered. Very rare.

1056 CHUBBUCK, S. W., TELEGRAPH CHEMICAL & PHILOSOPHICAL APPARATUS. R MORSE TELEGRAPH ALPHABET, the fourth line straight. Copper. 30m. Very rare.

1057 Same. Silver. Very rare.

1058 Same. Brass. Very rare.

1059 Same. W. M. Very rare.

1060 Same obverse. R fourth line curved. Silver.

1061 Same. Copper.

1062 Same. Brass.

1063 Same. White metal.

1064 KINGSLEY, T. L., GREAT WARDROBE CLOTHING. Brass. 29m.

1065 Same. Struck over 1863 token with Liberty seated. Brass.

1066 Same. Struck over United States cent.

WAVERLY.

1067 SEDGWICK, WAVERLY, N. Y. R Liberty bell. White metal.

WINDSOR.

1068 SMITH, C. A. M., GENERAL DEALER IN DRY GOODS, GROCERIES, &c. Copper. 28m.

YONKERS.

1069 BELL, A. Yonkers A. BELL 1857. Various scrolls, lines and other ornaments in the field. A. Bell in script letters struck over U. S. Cent. Unique.

NORTH CAROLINA.
WILMINGTON.

2　BAKER, W. & Co., WALNUT HILLS. ℞ Advertisement of Murdock & Spencer. Brass. 22m.

3　Similar, but from different die. ℞ Advertisement of John Stanton. Brass. 22m.

4　BEERS, C. H., REVOLVERS, CUTLERY, ETC., 550 BROADWAY, CINCINNATI. ℞ blank. Brass. 24m.

5　BILLIODS, F. BREWER. 25 CENTS IN BEER. ℞ Advertisement of John Stanton. Brass. 22m.

6　CREW'S PYRAMIDAL RAILWAY. CINCINNATI INDUSTRIAL EXPOSITION. 1871. AS A VELOCIPEDE. ℞ AS A STEAM CAR. White metal. 26m.

— 7　DODD, HATTER, CINCINNATI. Liberty head. ℞ Eagle. Brass.

8　DODD & CO. HATTERS. Similar. Brass.

9　Same. Copper.

10　Same. Brass, silvered.

—·11　ERWIN, S. C., HATTER, CINCINNATI. Eagle. ℞ Hat. Brass. 22m.

12　EVENS, P., DRAPER & TAILOR, CINCINNATI. Feuchtwanger metal. 24m. Rare.

13　Similar obverse, but different die. "BALE, N. Y." on obverse. Brass. Very rare.

14　FOSTER, J., JR. Brass.

15　EVENS SEWING MACHINES. German silver.

16　GRAY'S BANKRUPT STORE. ℞ GOOD FOR TEN CENTS. Advertisement of James Murdock, Jr., below. German silver. 19m.

17　KEMMETER, GEO. & CO. LOOKOUT HOUSE, JACKSON HILL. (Cincinnati) "5" on either side. Brass. 22m.

18　Similar, with "20." German silver. 22m.

19　KINSEY, E. & D., SILVERWARE MFGS. ℞ Exhibition Palace, London, 1851. Copper. 22m.

— 20a　Lamphears. Good for 25 cts. ℞ Blank. Brass. 22m.

21　McCLURE, E. A., Trader. ℞ Advertisement of Murdock & Spencer. Brass. 22m.

22　MURDOCK, JAMES, JR. ℞ NO. Brass. 22m.

23　ROSS, ALBERT, CINCINNATI. DRUGGIST. Brass. 21m.

24　Same. Nickel.

— 25　Same. White metal. Thick planchet.

26　Same. White metal. Thin planchet.

27　Same. White metal. Thick planchet. Reeded edge.

28　Same. Copper nickel.

29　SPENCER, WM. W. ℞ CINCINNATI INDUSTRIAL EXPOSITION. Thick planchet. Copper.

30　Same. White metal.

31　THOMAS & ROBINSON, DIES, &c. ℞ EXPOSITION BUILDING. 1870. White metal. 26m.

32　VARWIG, H., BAKER, CINCINNATI. 5 CTS. in BREAD. ℞ Advertisement of John Stanton. Brass. 22m.

33　WEIGHELL & SONS. EXCELSIOR TOBACCO WORKS. 20 CENTS IN TOBACCO. Copper. 22m.

34　WOOD & HARRISON. GOOD FOR 10 CENTS. ℞ Advertisement of John Stanton. Brass. 19½m.

35　ZANONI & BACCIOCCO, CINCINNATI. CHESS & WHIST CLUB. ℞ "5·" Brass. 22m.

CLEVELAND.

36 LOOMIS, A., CLEVELAND, OHIO, DEALER IN GROCERIES. LIQUORS, WINES, &c. No. 34 MERWIN ST., 1843. Eagle on obverse holds three links of chain in his beak. Talons hold two arrows, one pointing to right, the other left. Copper. (Low 158). Very rare.

37 Similar to last, but both arrows point to right. Copper. (Low 159). Very rare.

38 Similar to last, but three links are omitted from eagle's beak, and while the two arrows point to right they are out of a horizontal line. Copper. (Low 160). Very rare.

39 Obverse entirely different from last, with eleven stars above the eagle. ℞ a barrel in centre of field. Copper. Rare.

40 Similar to last, but entirely different die, and but six stars above eagle. ℞ same as last. Copper. Rare.

DAYTON.

41 RICKEY'S BOOK STORE, 326 3d St., DAYTON, O.— ℞ GO TO RICKEYS FOR BOOKS & PAPERS. 1863. CASH PAID FOR RAGS. Copper. 30m.

PENNSYLVANIA.

ALTOONA.

1 SCHROEDER, RUDOLPH, ALTOONA. ℞ Capitol. White metal.

BELLEFONTE.

PHILADELPHIA.

8   ALDRIDGE & EARP. A comb. Brass.

9   AMERICAN LIFE INSURANCE CO. ℞ Continental soldier. Copper.

10   Same obverse. ℞ Independence Hall. White metal.

11   Same. ℞ Liberty head. White metal.

12   Same as foregoing. Brass.

13   Same. ℞ Liberty bell. White metal.

14   Same. ℞ Maryland arms. White metal.

15   AHN'S, J. W., CONFECTIONERY, 1342 RIDGE AV., PHILA. ℞ Masonic Hall, Philadelphia. White metal. Small cent size.

16   Same obverse. ℞ Independence Hall. 1776. Small size. White metal.

17   Same obverse. ℞ Memorial Hall. 1876. Brass. Small size.

18   Same as foregoing. Copper.

19   ANGUE, A. D. Man with two umbrellas. Ins. in four lines. Brass.

20   Same. ℞ Ins. in three lines. Brass.

21   Similar. Man with four canes. Brass.

22   APPLEGATES GALLERIES. ℞ Capitol. White metal.

23   APPLEGATES PALACE OF FLYING ANIMALS. ℞ two donkeys. "When Shall We Three Meet Again?" Brass.

24   Same obverse. ℞ Liberty head. White metal.

25   Same obverse. ℞ Two heads. White metal.

26   APPLEGATES GALLERIES, VINE & 8th STS. ℞ blank. Small size. White metal.

27   APPLEGATE'S ON THE BEACH. ℞ blank. Small size. White metal.

28   BAILEY & CO. WATCHES, ETC. Gilt. Plain edge.

29   Same. Gilt. Reeded edge.

30   Same. Silvered. Plain edge.

31   Same. Silvered. Reeded edge.

32   Same. Brass.

33.   Same. Silver.

34   BAILEY, J. C. 1109 Spring Garden St. Boots & Shoes. Brass.

35   BARRY, C. M., SALOON, N. W. COR. 5TH & CHESTNUT, incused on Spanish 2 reales.

36   Similar counterstamp on old U. S. cent.

37   BARTON, ISAAC & CO DRY GOODS. Brass.

38   B. C. W. (C. W. Bender) 1842 Blank reverse. Feuchtwanger metal. Low 181.

39   Same. Silver. (Low 182).

40   BENDERS EATING SALOON. 6¼ cents. Brass.

41   Similar. 12 cents. Brass.

42   Similar. 19 cents. Brass.

43   Similar. 22 cents. Brass.

44   Similar. 25 cents. Brass.

45   Similar. 34 cents. Brass.

46   Similar. 35 cents. Brass.

47   Similar. 38 cents. Brass.

48   Similar. 44 cents. Brass.

49   Similar. 62½ cents. Brass.

50   BESTOR. S. J. WATCHES, etc. Washington on horseback. Silver.

51   Same. Copper.

52 Same. Silvered.

53 Same. ℞ Calendar. Brass.

54 BRIDESBURG BARREL MFG. CO. ℞ Plain. Brass. 32m.

55 Similar. ℞ "2." Brass.

56 Similar. ℞ "5." Brass.

57 Similar. ℞ "10." Brass.

58 Similar. ℞ "50." Brass.

59 BROWNING BROS. DRUGGISTS. ℞ Eagle. Brass.

60 BUEHLERS & SMITH. HARDWARE, Brass.

61 Same. Copper.

62 BURR & WITSILL. ℞ Capitol. White metal.

63 Same. ℞ Independence Hall. Copper.

64 Same as foregoing. White metal.

65 Same. ℞ Public Buildings. White metal.

66 Same. ℞ Liberty bell. White metal.

67 Same. ℞ Liberty head. White metal.

68 Same. ℞ Carpenters Hall. White metal.

69 Same. Brass. ?

70 Same. ℞ Continental soldier. Copper.

71 Same. ℞ Maryland arms. White metal.

72 BURWELL, WM. & BRO. CARRIAGE MOUNTINGS, ETC. ℞ Liberty head. White metal.

73 Same. ℞ Bell. White metal.

74 Same. ℞ Continental soldier. White metal.

75 Same. ℞ Maryland arms. White metal.

76 Same. Independence Hall. White metal. Maryland.

77 CASSIDY'S OLD ESTABLISHED STORE. ℞ Maryland arms. White metal.

78 Same. ℞ Continental soldier. White metal.

79 Same. ℞ Liberty head. White metal.

80 Same. ℞ Liberty bell. White metal.

81 Same. ℞ Carpenters Hall. White metal.

— 82 CATCH CLUB. Arms of Philadelphia. ℞ CATCH CLUB-12½ CENTS. Copper. 31m. Ex rare.

83 Same. Brass. 26m. Ex. rare.

84 Same. Silvered planchet. Reverse only. Ex. rare.

85 CENTENNIAL ADVERTISING MEDAL CO. 1020 CHESTNUT ST. PHILA. ℞ head of Washington. Small size. Copper.

86 Same as foregoing. White metal.

87 Same as foregoing. Copper-nickel.

88 CHAPMAN, W. B. ℞ Four names. German silver.

89 COGAN, EDWARD, 1859. ℞ Washington. Copper.

90 COGAN, EDWARD, 48 N. Tenth St. ℞ 1860. Copper. Reeded edge.

91 Same. ℞ Washington. White metal.

— 92 Same. Copper. Plain edge.

93 Same. Brass. Plain edge.

94 Same. Brass. Reeded edge.

95 Same. White metal. Reeded edge.

96 Same. White metal. Plain edge.

97 Same. Copper-nickel. Plain edge.

98 Same. Copper-nickel. Reeded edge.

99   Same. ℞ "The Highest Premium, etc." White metal.

100   Same. Brass.

101   Same. Copper.

102   Same. Copper-nickel.

103   CORPORATION OF PHILADELPHIA. Arms of the city. ℞ COR-
PORATION OF PHILADELPHIA. ONE SHILLING TOKEN. Feuchtwanger metal. 26m. Extremely rare. (Low 152).

104   COVERT, WM. NEWS EXCHANGE. ℞ Liberty head. White metal.

105   Same. ℞ Maryland arms. White metal.

106   Same. ℞ Continental soldier. White metal.

107   Same. ℞ Liberty bell. White metal.

108   Same. Copper.

109   CRAGIN, I. L. & CO. "Ask your grocer, etc." ℞ Liberty head. White
metal.

110   Same. "Make your grocer, etc." ℞ Pennsylvania arms. White metal.

111   Same. ℞ Liberty bell. White metal.

112   Same. ℞ Continental soldier. White metal.

113   Same. ℞ Liberty head. White metal.

114   DEPUY, THOMAS. ℞ Liberty head. White metal.

115   Same. ℞ Maryland arms. White metal.

116   Same. ℞ Liberty bell. Copper.

117   Same. Brass.

118   Same. ℞ Capitol. White metal.

119   Same. ℞ Independence Hall. White metal.

120   Same. ℞ Continental soldier. White metal.

121   Same. ℞ Carpenter Hall. White metal.

122   DICKSON, WHITE & CO. WATCHES. Brass.

123   Same. German silver.

124   DISSTON, HENRY, (Eagle.) PHILA. Struck on Spanish two reales.

125   DOBBINS, SOAP.

126   DOLL, GEO. & CO. ℞ Washington. Brass.

127   DROWN, WM. A. 86 MARKET ST. Umbrellas and Parasols. Brass.
Plain edge.

128   Same. Brass. Reeded edge.

129   DROWN, W. A. & CO. 246 MARKET ST. ℞ Date 1857 and names
of men composing the firm. Copper.

130   Same. Brass.

131   Same. White metal.

132   Same. Copper-nickel.

133   Same obverse. ℞ Date 1857 below umbrella. Copper.

134   Same. Brass.

135   Same. White metal.

136   Same. Copper-nickel.

137   Obverse same as reverse of last. ℞ Date 1857 and name of firm as
on No. 129. Copper.

138   Same. White metal.

139   Same. Brass.

140   Same. Copper-nickel.

141   Obverse same as preceding reverse. ℞ Blank Copper.

142 EVANS & WATSON, 304 CHESTNUT ST. ℞ Washington. Silver.
143 Same. Copper.
144 Same. Brass.
145 Same. White metal.
146 Same. Copper-nickel. . .
147 Same obverse. ℞ Ship, imitation of Sommer Island shilling reverse. Copper.
148 Same. Brass.
149 Same. White metal.
150 Same. Copper-nickel.
151 Same obverse. ℞ Hog, imitation of obverse of Sommer Island shiling. Copper.
152 Same. Brass.
153 Same. White metal.
154 Same. Copper-nickel.
155 Hog obverse combined with ship reverse, no mention of Evans & Watson. Copper.
156 Same. Brass.
157 Same. White metal.
158 Same. Copper-nickel.
159 Obverse, the Washington reverse. ℞ Ship. Copper.
160 Same. White metal.
161 Obverse the Washington rev. ℞ Hog. Copper.
162 F. S. 50 CENTS. ℞ Arms of Philadelphia. Feuchtwanger metal 26m. Extremely rare. (Low 149).
163 FEATHER, S. 12½ CENTS. ℞ Blank. Copper. 21m. Rare.
164 FLANAGAN, R. Punch. Copper.
165 Similar. Struck over Spanish two real piece. Very rare.
166 FLEMING, Dr. D. L. ℞ Capitol. White metal.
167 FRIES, MALSEED & HAWKINS. ℞ Liberty bell. Copper.
168 Same. Brass.
169 Same. White metal.
170 Same. ℞ Independence Hall. White metal.
171 FUSSELL, HENRY B. SUNSHADES. Brass
172 GERCKE, J. H. ℞ Liberty bell. White metal.
173 Same. ℞ Liberty head. White metal.
174 Same. ℞ Continental soldier. White metal.
175 Same. ℞ Maryland arms. White metal.
176 Same. ℞ Independence Hall. White metal.
177 Similar inscription, watches, checks, jewelry. Large size. White metal.
178 GILBERT, J. W., ℞ Liberty bell. Larger size. White metal.
179 GOODYEAR & SONS, BUTTONS, Patent Pitch Forks, etc. Brass. Extremely rare.
180 Same. Copper. Excessively rare.
181 GORDON, W. J. M. Western row & Eighth. ℞ Four names. German silver.
182 GREAT UNION PACIFIC TEA CO. "1 lb. COFFEE" ℞ Carpenters Hall. White metal.

183   Similar. "13." White metal.
184   Similar obverse has "15" ℞ Same as preceding. White metal.
185   Similar obverse has "18" ℞ Same as preceding. White metal.
186   Similar. ℞ Continental soldier. Large size. White metal.
187   HARBACH'S ORIGINAL WALNUT CANDY. ℞ Liberty bell. White metal.
188   Similar obverse, differing die. ℞ CENTENNIAL above Liberty bell, surmounted by eagle. White metal.
189   Same obverse. ℞ Liberty bell. Brass.
190   HARBACH'S CHRISTMAS TREE ORNAMENTS. ℞ Flag. White metal.
191   HARMSTEAD, JAMES. ℞ John Wesley. Brass.
192   Same. Copper.
193   HARRIS, T. B. SODA CHECK. ℞ Four names. German silver. Plain edge.
194   Same. Reeded edge
195   HART & CO. CLUB HOUSE CARDS. Silvered.
196-197 Same. Brass.
198   HART'S, 7th & CALLOWHILL, TEA STORE. ℞ Liberty bell. Copper.
199   Same. ℞ Liberty head. White metal.
200   Same. ℞ Continental soldier. White metal.
201   Same. ℞ Maryland arms. White metal.
202   HARVEY, SAMUEL & JOSEPH. HARDWARE, etc. Brass.
203   Same. Copper.
204   HOOPER, MARTIN & SMITH. 113 Market St. Brass.
205   Same. Copper.
206   HUGH'S HOUSE, 686 W. BROAD ST. Chris Hughes, Prop'r. ℞ Liberty head. White metal.
207   Same. ℞ Liberty bell. White metal.
208   Same. ℞ Continental soldier. White metal.
209   Same. ℞ Maryland arms. White metal.
210   IDLER, W. DEALER IN COINS, etc. ℞ Copy of obverse of Washington Half Dollar. Silver.
211   Same. Copper.
212   Same. Brass.
213   Same. ℞ Copy of reverse of Washington Half Dollar. Silver.
214   Same. Copper.
215   Same. Brass.
216   IDLER, W. Copy of Baltimore penny. Silver.
217   Same. Copper.
218   Same. Copper-nickel.
219   Same. Brass.
220   Same. Bronze.
221   Same. White metal, silvered.
222   Same. Nickel.
223   Obverse only of Baltimore penny. ℞ "Continental Paper Money, etc."
224   Copper. Reeded edge.
225   Same. Copper-nickel. Reeded edge.
226   Same. Copper-nickel. Plain edge.
227   Same. Brass. Plain edge.
228   Same. Brass. Reeded edge.
229   IDLER. W. ℞ Washington. Brass.
230   Same. White metal.

231 IRVINS E. Bust of Washington. ℞ Shield. Copper.
232 Same. Brass.
233 Same. White metal.
234 JACKSON, C. W. Coal dealer. Copper.
235 Same. Brass.
236 Same. ℞ "6." Brass.
237 Same. ℞ "25." Brass.
238 JONES EXCHANGE HOTEL. "12½ cents." Brass.
239 JONES EXCHANGE HOTEL, 77 DOCK ST. incuse on Spanish 2 rls.
240 KELLY'S FURNITURE, CARPETS, ETC. ℞ Independence Hall.
      Copper.
241 Same. White metal.
242 Same. ℞ Liberty head. Copper.
243 Same. White metal.
244 Same. ℞ Liberty bell. Copper.
245 Same. ℞ Carpenters Hall. Copper.
246 Same. ℞ Continental soldier. White metal.
247 Same. ℞ Maryland arms. White metal.
248 Same. ℞ Two heads conjoined. Copper.
249 KILBRIDE, G. DRUGGIST. ℞ Capitol. Copper.
250 Same. White metal.
251 Same. ℞ Independence Hall. White metal.
252 Same. Copper.
253 Same. ℞ Liberty bell. White metal.
254 Same. ℞ Liberty head. White metal.
255 Same. ℞ Continental soldier. White metal.
256 Same. Copper.
257 Same. ℞ Maryland arms. White metal.
258 KEY, F. C. & SONS. ℞ Wildey. Copper.
259 Same. White metal.
260 Same. ℞ Continental soldier. Brass.
261 Same. White metal.
262 Same. ℞ Kane. White metal.
263 Same. ℞ Odd Fellows Anniversary. White metal.
264 KEY, WM. H. & DIEHL. ℞ Head. Copper.
265 KEY & CO., 329 ARCH ST. ℞ Two heads. White metal.
266 Same. Brass.
267 Same. Copper.
268 Same. ℞ Forrest. White metal.
269 Same. ℞ Forrest, no inscription. White metal.
270 Same. ℞ Museum. White metal.
271 Same. ℞ Washington. Brass.
272 Same. ℞ Lyle. Brass.
273 Same. Copper.
274 Same. White metal.
275 Same. ℞ WE ALL HAVE OUR HOBBIES. Brass. Copper.
276 Same. Copper.
277 Same. White metal.
278 Same. ℞ DEDICATED TO COIN COLLECTORS. Brass.
279 Same. Copper.
280 Same. White metal.
281 Same. ℞ Cupid. Brass.

282   Same.   Copper.
283   Same.   White metal.
284   Same.   ℞ Surrender of General Lee.   Copper.
285   Same.   Brass.
286   KLINE, JOHN W.   ℞ Head of a Quaker.   Brass.
287   Same.   Copper.
288   Same.   White metal.
289   Same.   Silver.   Rare.
290   KNOPPEL, FREDERICK.   ℞ Liberty head.   White metal.
291   Same.   ℞ Maryland arms.   White metal.
292   Same.   ℞ Two heads.   Copper.
293   Same.   ℞ Continental soldier.   White metal.
294   LAMBERT, A. Cor. 4th & Library St.   ℞ Liberty head.   Brass.
296   LINGG & BRO. 304 So. 2nd St. Inner circle.   ℞ Watch.   Copper.   22m.
297   Same.   Brass.
298   Same.   White metal.
299   Same.   ℞ Independence Hall.   Copper.
300   Same.   ℞ Liberty head.   Copper.
301   LINGG & BRO. Without inner circle.   ℞ Liberty head.   White metal.
302   Same.   ℞ Two heads.   White metal.
303   Same.   ℞ Liberty bell.   White metal.
304   Same.   ℞ Public Buildings. Philadelphia.   White metal.
305   Same.   ℞ Carpenters Hall.   White metal.
306   Same.   ℞ Continental soldier.   White metal.
307   Same.   ℞ Maryland arms.   White metal.
308   Same.   ℞ Independence Hall   Brass.
309   Same.   White metal.
310   LINGG & BRO. Name in center.   ℞ Carpenters Hall.   White metal.
311   Same.   ℞ Two heads.   White metal.
312   Same.   ℞ Liberty head.   White metal.
313   Same.   ℞ Public Buildings.   White metal.
314   LINGG & BRO. COMMEMMORATION JULY 5, 1875, in scroll.   ℞ Continental soldier.   Brass.
315   Same.   Copper.
316   Same obverse.   ℞ Independence Hall.   Brass.
317   Same obverse.   ℞ Liberty head.   White metal.
318   LINGG & CO. Mfgs. of Metallic Business Cards, etc.   ℞ Liberty bell.   White metal.
319   Same.   Brass.
320   Same.   Copper.
321   Same.   ℞ Capitol.   Copper.
322   Same.   ℞ Independence Hall.   White metal.
323   Same.   ℞ Liberty head.   White metal.
324   Same.   ℞ Continental soldier.   White metal.
325   Same.   Copper. Maryland.
326   Same.   ℞ Maryland arms.   White metal.
327   LONG, WM. W. Refectory.   Copper.
328   Same.   Silver.   Very rare.
329   Same.   Brass.   Rare.
330   LOVETT, R. JR.   ℞ Statue of Stephen Girard.   White metal.   Plain edge.
331   Same.   Reeded edge.

3 2   Same. Brass Plain edge.
3 3   Same. Reeded edge. Brass.
3 4   Same. Copper. Plain edge.
3 5   Same. Copper. Reeded edge.
336   Same. Copper-nickel. Plain edge.
      Both thick and thin planchets of the preceding.
337-338 Same. ℞ Washington on horseback. Brass. Plain edge.
339   Same. Brass. Reeded edge.
340   Same. White metal. Reeded edge.
341   Same. White metal. Plain edge.
342   Same. Copper. Reeded edge.
343   Same. Nickel. Reeded edge.
344-345 Same. ℞ Naval battle. White metal.
346   LOVETT, R. JR. ℞ Minerva. 1858. Copper.
347   Same. White metal.
348   LOVETT, R. JR. ℞ St. George slaying dragon. German silver.
349   Same. Copper.
350   Same. Brass.
351   Same. White metal.
352   Same. Copper-nickel. . .
353   LOVETT, R. JR. 1860 Confederate cent obverse. Copper.
354   Same. Brass.
355   Same. Copper-nickel.
356   Same. Nickel.
357   MALSEED & HAWKINS, CLOTH HOUSE. ℞ Liberty. White metal.
358   Same. ℞ Liberty bell. White metal.
359   Same. ℞ Continental soldier. White metal.
360   Same. ℞ Maryland arms. White metal.
361   Same. ℞ Capitol. Copper.
362   Same. White metal.
363   MASON & CO. ℞ Washington. White metal.
364   Same. Copper.
365   Same. Brass.
366   Same. Copper-nickel.
367   MORGAN & ORR. 1855 Copper.
368   Same. White metal.
369   Same. Nickel.
370   MULLIGAN, H. Watches, etc. ℞ Eagle. Brass. 32m.
371   Same. Copper.
372   Same. Silver. Rare.
373   Same. White metal.
374   MURPHY, D. M. 2nd & CHRISTIAN STS "15" ℞ Carpenters Hall.
      White metal.
375   Similar. Smaller letters. "20" ℞ Same as preceding. White metal.
376   MURPHY, D. M. 1 lb. COFFEE in centre. ℞ Liberty head. White
      metal.
377   Same obverse. ℞ Carpenters Hall. White metal.
378   NEEDLES, C. H. Soda check. Copper-nickel.
379   Same. White metal.
380   OMNIBUS LINE, 6th & 8th Sts. Line. An omnibus to r. Brass.
381   P. P. P. Brass.
382   PARTRIDGE & RICHARDSON. Horseman to r. ℞ Bee hive. Brass.

383 PENNSYLVANIA MUTUAL LIFE INSURANCE CO. ℞ Liberty bell. Copper.
384 Same. White metal.
385 Same. ℞ Maryland arms. White metal.
386 Same. ℞ Liberty head. White metal.
387 Same. ℞ Continental soldier. White metal.
388 Same. ℞ Carpenters Hall. White metal.
389 Same. ℞ Capitol. White metal.
390 PENNYPACKER & SIBLEY. ℞ "25" Brass.
391 Same. Copper.
392 PEAELZER BROS. WHOLESALE JEWELRY. ℞ Independence Hall. Copper.
394 PHILADELPHIA MUSEUM. Bust of Charles Wilson Peale, founder 1784. ℞ Wreath. Copper.
395 Similar. Number in wreath. Copper.
396 Same. Gilt.
397 Similar. Within wreath.—ADMIT THE BEARER. Silver.
398 Same. Copper.
399 PIC-NICK & SOMMERNACHTSFEST, etc. ℞ Lincoln by Bolen. White metal. 26m.
400 PICARD, A. Watches & Jewelry. ℞ Liberty bell. Brass.
401 Same. White metal.
402 Same obverse. ℞ Independence Hall. White metal.
403 Same obverse. ℞ Liberty head. White metal.
404 RECH, JACOB. CARRIAGE & WAGON BUILDER. ℞ Lincoln by Bolen. White metal. 26m.
405 REED, J. ℞ Liberty bell. White metal.
406 Same. Copper.
407 Same. ℞ Independence Hall. White metal.
408 Same. ℞ Liberty head. White metal.
409 Same. ℞ Continental soldier. White metal.
410 Same. ℞ Maryland arms. White metal.
411 RICE, M. H. ℞ Continental soldier. White metal.
412 Same. ℞ Maryland arms. White metal.
413 Same. ℞ Liberty head. White metal.
414 Same. ℞ Liberty bell. White metal.
415 Same. ℞ Carpenters Hall. White metal.
416 RICHARDSON, W. & C. 106 MARKET ST. An umbrella. Brass.
417 RICHARDSON, W. H. 5 SOUTH 4th ST. ℞ Three umbrellas. Brass. Reeded edge.
418 Same. Plain edge.
419 Same. Copper. Plain edge.
420 Same. Silvered. Plain edge.
421 RICHARDSON, WM. H. 418 MARKET ST. Brass. 24m.
422 RICHARDSON, W. H., 807 MARKET ST. Umbrellas and canes, crossed. Brass. 24m.
423 RICHARDSON, W. H. 104 MARKET ST. Umbrellas. Brass. Plain edge.
424 Same. Reeded edge.
425 Same. Copper.
426 Similar. Without ornaments on obverse or reverse. Brass. Reeded edge.

427 Same. Brass. Plain edge.
428 RICKETT'S CIRCUS. Silver. Reeded edge. Rare.
429 Same. Bronze. Reeded edge. Rare.
430 Same. Copper. Plain edge. Very thick planchet. Rare.
431 ROOT, M. A. 140 CHESTNUT ST. ℞ Eagle. Brass. Reeded edge.
432 Same. Copper. Reeded edge.
433 ROOT, M. A. Same obverse. ℞ FIRST PREMIUM, etc. Brass. Reeded
       edge.
434 Same. Brass. Plain edge.
435 Same. Brass, silvered.
436 Same. Copper.
437 ROOT, M. A. Similar but address 144 Chestnut St. Brass.
438 SAUSSER, DANGLER & CO. ℞ Liberty head. White metal.
439 Same. ℞ Continental soldier. White metal.
440 Same. ℞ Liberty bell. White metal.
441 Same. ℞ Maryland arms. White metal.
442 Same. ℞ Independence Hall White metal.
443 SCHMIDT, JOHN K. 1236 Poplar St. An awl. Brass.
444 Same. Copper.
445 Same. White metal.
446 Same obverse. ℞ Public buildings. Brass.
447 Same. White metal.
448 Similar obverse, awl in field. Brass.
449 SCOTT, C. B. & CO. ℞ Liberty head. White metal.
450 Same. Brass.
451 Same. ℞ Independence Hall. Brass.
452 Same. White metal.
453 Same. ℞ Continental soldier. White metal.
454 Same. ℞ Liberty bell. White metal.
455 Same. ℞ Maryland arms. White metal.
456 SERVER, JOHN H. ℞ Liberty bell. White metal.
457 Same. ℞ Liberty head. White metal.
458 Same. ℞ Continental soldier. White metal.
459 Same. ℞ Maryland arms. White metal.
460 Same. ℞ Independence Hall. White metal.
461 Same. ℞ Two heads. White metal.
462 SHAMGAR & HARD. ℞ Liberty bell. Copper.
463 Same. Brass.
464 Same. White metal.
465 Same. ℞ Liberty head. White metal.
466 Same. ℞ Continental soldier White metal.
467 Same. ℞ Maryland arms. White metal.
468 Same. ℞ Independence Hall. White metal.
469 SHARPLESS BROS. Dry Goods. A bee hive. Brass.
470 Same. Nickel (German silver).
471 Same. Gilt.
472 Same. Silvered.
473 Same. White metal.
474 Same. Silver.
475 SLEEPER & FENNER. Umbrellas. An umbrella and parasol. Brass.
476 Same. Liberty head. ℞ Eagle. Brass. Reeded edge.
477 Same. Copper. Plain edge.

478   Same. Silvered.
479   SMITH & BROTHER. Hardware. Brass.
480   SMITH, JAMES R. Dry Goods. Brass.
481   SMITH, MURPHY & CO. Dry Goods. Brass.
482   SMITH, MURPHY CO. ℞ James Harris. Brass.
483   SNYDER & SHANKLAND. Tailors. Copper. 32m. Rare.
484   Same. Brass. Rare.
485   Same. White metal. Rare. |
486   SPERING, GOOD & CO. 138 Market St. Brass. 33m. Rare.
487   Same. Silvered. Rare.
488   SPERING, MIXSELL & INNESS, Same address as preceding. Brass.
489   STEEL, ROBERT, 815 Chestnut St. "30." German silver.
490   STEVENS, A. M. ℞ Four names. German silver.
491   STILZ, JOHN & SON. ℞ Liberty head. Copper.
492   Same. White metal.
493   Same. ℞ Liberty bell. White metal.
494   Same. ℞ Independence Hall. White metal.
495   Same. ℞ Continental soldier. White metal.
496   Same. ℞ Maryland arms. White metal.
497   Same. ℞ Capitol. White metal.
498   STOKES, GRANVILLE. Clothing. 609 Chestnut St. Brass.
499   Same. White metal.
500   STOKES, CO., 607 CHESTNUT ST. ℞ blank section of Atlantic cable.
501   STOLTZ'S SEGAR STORE PHILADA. Struck over Spanish two reales.
502   STOUGHTON, DR. ℞ Capitol. White metal.
503   SUIVE, ECKSTEIN & CO. DRUGGISTS. German silver.
504   TAYLOR, A.B. SODA WATER 1860. ℞ THE BEST PREPARATION,
           etc. German silver..
505   Same. ℞ A FULL ASSORTMENT etc. German silver.
506   Same obverse. ℞ Eagle. Copper.
507   TAYLOR, A.B. DRUGGIST & APOTHECARY. ℞ THE BEST. etc.
           Copper-nickel.
508   Same. Copper.
509   Same. ℞ A FULL etc. Copper-nickel.
510   Same. Copper.
511   Same. German silver.
512   TAYLOR, APOTHECARY. 1015 CHESTNUT ST. ℞ Same as preced-
           ing. Copper.
513   TAYLOR, N. G., & CO., PHILADELPHIA, 303 BRANCH ST. (Gothic
           letters). TIN PLATE, METALS, FILES, &c. Reeded edge. Brass.
           Size 38mm. (Roman letters). '
514   Same obverse. ℞ similar, but different spacing of letters. Brass.
515   Same as foregoing. Tin.
516   Similar to 513, but inscription in Gothic letters. Dated 1862. ℞ TIN
           PLATE, WIRE, SHEET IRON, &c., in Gothic letters. Brass.
517   Similar to foregoing, but inscription on reverse differently spaced. The
           "E" in "JAPANNED" close to "&." Brass .

       NOTE—There is another card bearing the name of this firm, of size
       25, which is listed with the civil war tokens.

518 THOMAS J. KOSSUTH'S EX. PHILADA. Struck over Spanish two reales.

519 THORNTON, JAMES. Looking Glass, Picture & Bracket Depot. ℞ Liberty bell. Copper.

520 Same. White metal.

521 Same. ℞ Liberty head. White metal.

522 Same. ℞ Continental soldier. White metal.

523 Same. ℞ Maryland arms. White metal.

524 VALLEE, JOHN E. ℞ Independence Hall. White metal.

525 Same. ℞ Carpenters Hall. White metal.

526 Same. ℞ Liberty head. White metal.

527 Same. ℞ Liberty bell. White metal.

528 Same. ℞ Continental. soldier. White metal.

529 Same. ℞ Maryland arms. White metal.

530 WATSON, JAMES, HARDWARE. Copper, gilt.

531 Same. Brass.

532 WANAMAKER & BROWN. Flag. ℞ Oak Hall. Brass.

533 WARNER, CHARLES K. Small bust of Washington. ℞ 28 Battles. Copper.

534 Same. Brass.

535 Same. White metal.

536 Same. ℞ General Peter Lyle. Copper.

537 Same. Brass.

538 Same. White metal.

539 Same. ℞ The Constitution & the Union. Copper.

540 Same. Brass.

541 Same. White metal.

542 Same. ℞ General U. S. Grant. Copper.

543 Same. Brass.

544 Same. White metal.

545 Same. ℞ Surrender of General Lee. Copper.

546 Same. Brass.

547 Same. White metal.

548 Same. ℞ Horatio Seymour. Copper.

549 Same. Brass.

550 Same. White metal.

551 Same. ℞ Monitor 1862. Copper.

552 Same. Brass.

553 Same. White metal.

554 Same. ℞ Abraham Lincoln. Copper.

555 Same. Brass.

556 Same. White metal.

557 Same. ℞ Head of Washington on flags. Copper.

558 Same. Brass.

559 Same. White metal.

560 Same. ℞ General George B. McClellan. Copper.

561 Same. Brass.

562 Same. White metal.

563 Same. ℞ Differing head of McClellan. Copper.

564 Same. Brass.

565 Same. White metal.

566 Same. ℞ Victoria and Albert of England. Copper.

567 Same. Brass.
568 Same. White metal.
569 Same. ℞ Flag. Brass.
570 WEIDNER, A. J. Lamps, etc. ℞ Liberty head. White metal.
571 Same. ℞ Liberty bell. White metal.
572 Same. ℞ Continental soldier. White metal.
573 Same. ℞ Maryland arms. White metal.
574 WHITE, W. H. & Co. Watches. Copper.
575 WHITMAN & SON. ℞ Maryland arms. White metal.
576 Same. ℞ Liberty bell. White metal.
577 Same. ℞ Liberty head. White metal.
578 Same. ℞ Continental soldier. White metal.
579 WILLIAMS, DR. ℞ Independence Hall. Copper.
580 WILLIAMS, F. G. & Co. Anti Dyspeptic Elixir. ℞ Liberty head.
      White metal.
581 Same. ℞ Liberty bell. White metal.
582 Same. ℞ Continental soldier. White metal.
583 Same. ℞ Maryland arms. White metal.
584 WINE STORE, 96 North 3rd St. Bunch of Grapes. ℞ Blank. Brass.
585 WOODS MUSEUM, 9th and Arch. ℞ Liberty head. Brass.
586 Same. White metal.
587 YATES, A. C. & CO. 6th & Chestnut Sts. ℞ Eagle. Brass.
588 Similar. Without eagle. Brass.

PITTSBURGH.

589 CO-METALLIC DOLLAR OF EUTOPIA. Gold insert. 1886. Silver
      and gold. Very rare.
590 MORSE'S LITERARY DEPOT. A lamp. Copper.
591 STEVENSON, W. WATCHMAKER AND JEWELER. ℞ Blank. 32m.
592 Same. Copper.

SCRANTON.

593 SCRANTON STOVE WORKS. Copper.

SUNBURY.

594 SIMON OPPENHEIMER, CLOTHING. ℞ Carpenters Hall. White
      metal.

TYRONE.

595 EINTRACHT. Monogram. ℞ 10 in wreath. German silver.

RHODE ISLAND.

NEWPORT.

1 PORTER, S., 32 HIGH ST., MERCHANT TAILOR. Brass.

PROVIDENCE.

2 CLARK & ANTHONY. '1835' JEWELER. ℞ Lafayette standing.
      Copper. (Low 94).
3 FINCK, GEORGE, Rochester Hotel. Head of Washington. White
      metal. 22m.

— 4 HANDY, W. A., MERCHANT TAILOR. ℞ Eagle. Copper. (Low 78).
— 5 HATHAWAY, EPHRAIM A., CITY COAL YARD. ℞ Fire grate. Copper. (Low 74).
6 SMITH, S., PROV., R. I. "20" in centre. ℞ MERCHANTS SALOON. "20" in centre. White metal. 28m.
7 Same. "21." White metal.
8 Same. "24." White metal.
9 Same. "30." White metal.
10 Same. "37." White metal.
11 Same. "40." White metal.
12 Same. "43." White metal.
13 Same. "75." White metal.
14 Same. "93." White metal.
15 Same. "95." White metal.
16 Same. "100." White metal.
17 Similar inscription. Brass. Various figures. "18." 22m.
18 Same. "68." Brass.
19 PLASTRIDGE, A. A., PROV. R. I. "MERRIAM" within inner ring. ℞ WHAT CHEER EATING HOUSE. White metal. 27m.
20 Same obverse, but "R. D. 6" within shield in center. ℞ "12 G" in shield. "WHATCHEER BAGATELLE TABLES." White metal. 27m.
21 PROVIDENCE INSTITUTION FOR SAVINGS. ℞ PRESENT THIS CHECK, &c. White metal. 27m.

SOUTH CAROLINA.

CHARLESTON.

1 BAKER, R. L., Soda Check, Feuchtwanger metal. (Low 108). Excessively rare.
2 BARUC, BERNARD S., IMPORTER OF FANCY GOODS & TOYS, 203 KING STREET. ℞ Eagle and design similar to spiel mark of Strassburger & Nuhn of New York. Copper. Excessively rare.
2a Same. Brass. Excessively rare.
3 HAVILAND, STEVENSON & CO. Wholesale Druggists. ℞ Eagle on mortar. Copper. 28m.
4 Same. Brass.
5 WILBUR, W. W., AUCTIONEER, 1846. Auctioneer with hammer, ℞ Palmetto tree. Brass. No period after "CA"
6 Same. Feuchtwanger metal. Very rare. Period after "CA."
— 7 Same. Copper.
8 Same. Brass.
— 9 Similar. GOING AT ONLY A PENNY below auctioneer. Brass.
10 Same. Copper.
11 Same. German silver. Extremely rare.
12 Same. No period after "C A" Copper.
13 Same. Brass.

COLUMBIA.

14 SEEGERS, J. C. & CO. Barrel in field. ℞ "25." German silver.

TENNESSEE.

COAL CREEK.

1   COAL CREEK MINING CO., COAL CREEK, TENN. ℞ "500." Nickel.
2   Same. "100." Nickel. Ornament below "100." Nickel.
3   Same. Word MERCHANDISE below "100." Nickel.
4   Same. "50·" Ornament below "50." Nickel.
5   Same. "25·" Nickel.
6   Same. "10." Nickel.
7   Same. "5." Nickel.

MEMPHIS.

8   CLEAVES, C. C., BOOKSELLER. Brass. 26m.
9   FARGASON, CORDES & CO. Drayage Check. "50." Brass. 22m.
10 Same. "25·" Brass. 22m.
11 FRANCISCO & CO., HATTERS. ℞ "348 MAIN ST." Copper. Plain
    edge.
12 Same. Brass. Reeded edge.
13 Same. Brass, silvered.
14 Same obverse. ℞ "289 MAIN ST." Brass.
15 Same obverse. ℞ Bust of Kossuth. Brass.
16 Same. White metal.
17 Same obverse. ℞ DODD, CINCINNATI. Copper.
18 Same. Brass.
19 Obverse "289 MAIN ST., MEMPHIS, TENN." ℞ Padlock. Copper.
20 FRANCISCO & WIGGIN, HATTERS, ℞ PEABODY HOTEL, 307 MAIN
    ST."
21 Copper. Plain edge.
22 Same. Copper. Reeded edge.
23 Same. Brass. Plain edge.
24 Same. White metal.
25 Same. White metal, thick planchet. Plain edge.
26 HALLER & ELLIS, Betts 211.
27 HARRIS, A. O., & CO., MEMPHIS, TENN. "50 DRAYAGE." Brass
    26m.
28 KOHN DARON & CO. ℞ GOOD FOR ONE LOAD." Brass. 27m.
29 MEGIBBEN & BRO., MEMPHIS. "50" DRAYAGE." Brass. 25m.
30 MERRILL, J. M., & CO. 25 CENTS. Brass.
31 MEMPHIS JOCKEY CLUB, 1858. In the field a jockey on horseback.
    ℞ blank. Oval. Brass. 40x32m. Very rare.
32 MILLER, M. H., & CO. HATTERS. ℞ Liberty head. Brass
33 Same obverse. ℞ Eagle. Brass.
34 Same. Silver. Very rare.
35 NEVILS & ROSE, MEMPHIS. "50 DRAYAGE." Brass. 25m.
36 PAUL & CROCKETT. Betts 211.
37 SHEERER, J. W., & CO. ℞ DRAYAGE 10 CENTS. Brass. 30½m.
38 Same. "15 CENTS."
39 Same. "20 CENTS."
40 Same. "25 CENTS."
41 Same. "50 CENTS."
42 S. McD & CO. ℞ "25 CENTS." Brass.

43 SOUTHWORTH & KNIGHT. "50 DRAYAGE." Brass. 26m.
44 TARBOX, N. Y., & Co., CHURCH ST. ℞ blank. Brass. Reeded edge. 23m.
45 T. C. & CO. NO. 230. "50 DRAYAGE." Brass. 26m.
46 WESTERN FOUNDRY. "25" in centre. Brass.
47 WISWELL, J. M., & CO. "25 CENTS." ℞ blank. Brass. 28m.
48 WILSON, LAIRD & CO. MEMPHIS. "50 DRAYAGE." Brass. 26m.
49 Same. "25." Brass. 26m.
50 WOLF, M., DRAYAGE CHECK. "25." Brass.
51 Same. "50." Brass. 26m.
52 W. H. & CO. Brass. Betts 213.

NASHVILLE.

53 FRANCISCO & WHITMAN, HATTERS, Eagle. ℞ Hat. Brass. Reeded edge.
54 Same. Brass, silvered.
55 Same. Copper. Plain edge.
56 Same obverse. ℞ FRANCISCO & CO. Brass.
57 Same obverse. ℞ Lincoln. Tin.
58 HARRIS & PEARL, NASHVILLE. ℞ Drayage 5 Cents. White metal.
59 KIRKHAM, H. & I. Copper. Extremely rare.
60 Same. Silver. Unique.
61 SINGLETON, R. H., BOOKSELLER. ℞ Lincoln. Copper-nickel. Excessively rare.

VERMONT.

CHELSEA.

1 GUSTIN & BLAKE. Tin, Copper and Sheet Iron Workers. ℞ Tea pot. Copper. Low 175. Rare.
2 Similar. Dies recut. Low 176. Copper. Rare.

VIRGINIA.

ALEXANDRIA.

1 PIEPENBRING, E. ℞ "Good for 3 Cents." Brass. Rare.

DANVILLE.

2 COLE & FLINN. ℞ Liberty bell. White metal.

LYNCHBURG.

3 DIAMOND SALOON, 65 9th St. ℞ Liberty head. Brass. 20m.
4 PIEDMONT CLUB. Shield in centre. ℞ "10" in wreath. German silver. 20m.
5 RAINE, CHARLES J. CLOTHING. ℞ Eagle. Brass.

NORFOLK.

6   BARCLAY, R. C. BOOKSELLER. Copper.
7   Same. Brass.
8   BOTSFORD, S. N. CLOCKS, etc. Face of a clock. Copper.
9   CHAMBERLAINE, R. "Parties Supplied at Short Notice." White metal.
10 Same. ℞ Washington. White metal.
11 Same. ℞ Apollo. White metal. Obverse of Hess & Speidel card, Boston.
12 Same obverse. ℞ Plain. White metal. Said to have been but 2 struck.
13 Same. ℞ MADE FROM COPPER, etc. Copper. Rare.

PETERSBURG.

14 CITY OF PETERSBURG. ℞ Dog. Brass.
15 MARKS & CO. ℞ Liberty head. White metal.
16 Same. ℞ Penn. arms. White metal.
17 Same. ℞ Liberty bell. White metal.
18 WOLFF, JAMES E. HATTER. ℞ Wolf. Copper. Plain edge.
19 Same. Copper. Reeded edge.
20 Same. Brass. Plain edge.
21 Same. Copper nickel. Reeded edge.
22 Same. German silver. Plain edge.
23 Same. Reeded edge.
24 Same. White metal. Plain edge.
25 Same. White metal. Reeded edge.
26 Same. ℞ Shield. Copper-nickel.
27 Same White metal.
28 Same. ℞ Flag. Copper-nickel.
29 Same. Silver. Rare.

RICHMOND.

30 BECK'S PUBLIC BATHS. Nude female. Copper.
31 Same. White metal. Very rare.
32 Same. Feuchtwanger metal. Ex. rare.
33 MORGENSTERN, O. ℞ 5. Brass. Two dies.
34 Same. ℞ similar but different die. Brass.
35 Same. ℞ 10. German silver.
36 PIZZINI. CONFECTIONERS, 807 BROAD STREET. ℞ Capitol. White metal.
37 Same. ℞ Continental soldier. White metal.
38 SAUER, C. RICHMOND, Va. ℞ Eagle. Brass.
39 Same. 5 incuse on obverse. Brass.
40 Same. 10 incuse on obverse. Brass.
41 Same. 25 incuse on obverse. German silver.
42 SCHAEFER, CHRIST. ELBA PARK. ℞ 5. Brass.
43 Same. ℞ 10. Brass.
44 WARING, W. L., DRUGGIST. ℞ ONE SODA etc. stamped on crude white metal planchet.

WISCONSIN.

MILWAUKEE.

1 BYRON, W. H. & CO. HARDWARE. Eagle. ℞ Liberty head. Brass. Rare.
2 HOPKINS, I. A. 1850. BOOKSELLER. ℞ Eagle. Brass.
3 Same. Copper.
4 Similar. No date. Brass.
5 Same. Copper.
6 Same. Brass, silvered.
7 KLEINSTEUBER, CHRIS. 1863. 24 Tamarach St. Copper.
8 Similar. 1867. 318 State St. White metal.
9 SMITH, J. McD. COR OF MAIN & DETROIT STS. Copper. Extremely rare. 28m.

RACINE.

10 VAN COTT, A.B. JEWELRY. Eagle. ℞ Clock face. Brass. Thick planchet.
11 Same. Brass. Thin planchet.
12 Same. Copper.
13 Similar. RACIM (error) Brass.

· END.

Reprinted from Numismatic Scrapbook Magazine

Issue of May, 1954.

Adam's "United States Store Card" Index

MELVIN FULD, Baltimore 9, Maryland

GEORGE FULD, Cambridge 29, Mass.

*EDWARD H. DAVIS, Waterbury 10, Conn.

Adam's "United States Store Cards" is a "list of Merchants' Advertising Checks, Restaurant Checks, and kindred pieces issued from 1789 up to recent years (1920) including many of the tokens which passed as money and known as Hard Times Tokens."

It must be recognized that due to the extensive nature of such a large field that there are bound to be many omissions from Adams' list. Adams intended to revise this list but never did so.

Adams in his introduction to his book stated, "The small tradesmen's tokens issued during the Civil War from 1861 to 1864 inclusive, are not included in this list, but will be made the subject of another list, which will be published later." This list was later published by Hetrich-Guttag in 1924 and this list will be a subject of another paper which will appear in the Numismatic Scrapbook Magazine shortly.

In general, the arrangement is alphabetic, regardless of location. As a rule, reverses are listed as well as obverses. Where initials only are listed, they are placed under both the first letter and the last, as well as under the surname when known.

Practice varies in presenting the State and Number. Usually, only the first number of a sequence is given, but when the sequence covers significant variation in design the full range of numbers is indicated. Reappearance of a title in scattered locations is indicated by a series of numbers in a given state or by a succession of lines for different states.

There has been no attempt to include the numerous other early store cards unlisted in Adams.

This list is offered for two purposes; — to locate a coin carrying no address: and to furnish an all-over check list of representative names, particularly for people not having the book, which is now out of print.

---

*This index was proposed and initated by Mr. Davis in the course of his research among the many store cards made by the Scovill Manufacturing Co.

State No.

Mo. 40—Abraham, M. A.

Md. 2—Accommodation Line

Mass. 131—Adams, John J.

N.Y. 41—Admit
(Park Theater, N.Y.)
Pa. 15—Ahn's, J. W. Confectionery
La. 1—Albert, J. J.
La. 2—Albert & Trecon
Pa. 8—Aldredge and Earp
N.Y. 42—Alexander Herr
N.J. 26—Allers, George
Pa. 9—American Life Insurance Co.
Ill. 44—Amsden, N. C.
Md. 3—Anchor Hotel
N.Y. 43—Anderson, Henry
(Low 107)
Pa. 19—Angue, A. D.
Mo. 1—Anheuser Busch Brewing
Assn.
Mass. 4—Apollo Garden
Pa. 22—Applegates Galleries
Pa. 23—Applesgates Flying Animals
Pa. 27—Applegates On the Beach
N.Y. 44—Ashton, S., American Inn
N.Y. 45—Atwood's Railroad Hotel
N.Y. 49—Austin, C.
Mass. 18—Ayer, Wells W.
Pa. 28—Bailey & Co.
Pa. 34—Bailey, J. C.
N.Y. 50—Bailly Ward and Co.
Ill. 4—Baker and Moody
S.C. 1—Baker, R. L.   (Low 108)
Ohio 2—Baker W. and Co.
Ohio 1—Baker Wm. and Co.
Md. 1—Baker, W. R.
Mass. 19—Baker, Wright and
Howard
Ohio 13—Bale
N.Y. 61—Bale and Smith
Mich. 7—Ball, Daniel & Co.
N.Y. 55—Baltimore & Ohio R.R.
Md. 11—Baltimore, E. St. 33 & 35
(J. Beard)
Md. 7—Baltimore Token
N.Y. 56—Bancroft Redfield & Rice
Va. 6—Barclay, R. C.
N.Y. 57—Barker, John
Md. 10—Barnes, S. C. & Co.
N.J. 27—Barnett's Malleable & Gray
Iron
N.Y. 58—Barnum's Museum
Pa. 35—Barry, C. M.
Pa. 37—Barton, Isaac & Co.

S.C. 2—Baruc, Bernard S.
Conn. 14—Bassett & Co.
Pa. 38—B. C. W. (C. W. Bender)
(Low 181)
Mass. 20—Beals, J. J. & W.
Va. 30—Becks Public Baths
Ohio 4—Beers, C. H.
N.Y. 1069—Bell, A.
Md. 12—Belt, Wm. and Co.
Pa. 38—Bender
Pa. 40—Bender's Eating Saloon
Conn. 28—Benedict & Burnham
(Low 109)
N.Y. 60—Benziger Bros.
Cal. 3—Berenhart Jacoby & Co.
N.J. 1—Bergen Iron Works
(Low 143)
Pa. 50—Bestop, S. J.
Conn. 20—Betts, C. W.
Md. 182—B.F.Z. & Co. Citizens Line
Md. 13—Bibb (BC)
Ohio 5—Billiods, F.
Md. 5—B. L. monogram
(Balto Liederkranz)
N.Y. 65—Black, Friend &
N.Y. 61-4—Black, S. H.
N.Y. 66-8—Black, Samuel H.
Md. 15—Block (Edw'd) & Co.
N.J. 10—Bodine Bros.
Mo. 4—Bohennan Dr.
Mass. 121-25—Bolen, J. A.
N.Y. 69—Bollhagen, Theodore & Co.
N.Y. 73-4—Bondy Brothers & Co.
Va. 8—Botsford, S. N.
Conn. 2—Botsford S.N. & H. C.
N.Y. 1035—Boutwell O. & P.
(Low 87)
N.Y. 75—Bowen & McNamee
Md. 187—Bowman, G. R.
Mass. 25a—Bradford, M. L. & Co.
N.Y. 79—Bradley, Jas. S.
N.Y. 80—Bradstreet Hoffman & Co.
N.Y. 80—Bradstreet, J. M. & Sons
N.J. 28—Bragan, E & I
Maine 1—Bragg, N. H. & Son
N.Y. 83—Brewster, J. & L.
Pa. 54—Bridesburg Barrel Mfg. Co.
Mass. 99—Brigham, Francis L.
(Low 73)

N.Y. 87-133—Brimelow, T.
Brogan — see Bragan
N.Y. 7—Brooklyn Rink
Md. 16—Brooks, Geo. D.
Mich. 1—Brown Bros.
Conn. 29—Brown & Bros.
Ky. 1—Brown Curtis & Vance
N.Y. 134—Brown H. & Co.
N.Y. 1024—Brown W. R.
Pa. 59—Browning Bros.
N.Y. 1023—Brunk, Frank M.
N.Y. 137—Buchan, David C.
Md. 17—Buck, G. W.
N.Y. 1037-44—Bucklin's Book-Keeping (Low 77)
Pa. 60—Buehlers and Smith
Md. 9—B U P Ry. Co.
Ill. 8—Burbank and Shaw
Pa. 62—Burr and Witsill
Mo. 2—Burrows & Jennings
Pa. 72—Burwell, Wm. & Bro.
N.Y. 141—Byrne, Eleanor Rugg
N.Y. 141—Byrneore Gold
Wis. 1—Byron, W. H. & Co.
Md. 19—Calf Hide Assoc. of Balto.
Md. 21—Calverton Club
N.Y. 1045—Carpenter & Mosher
(Low 145)
N.Y. 144—Carrington & Co.
Md. 23—Carrollton Clothing House
Md. 24—Casino No. 3
Pa. 77—Cassidy's Old Established
Store
Pa. 82—Catch Club
Conn. 20—Celluloid Starch Co.
Pa. 83—Centennial Advertising
Medal Co.
N.Y. 148—Center Market (Low 110)
Md. 27—Central Pass R.R. Co.
Md. 26—Central Railway Co.
Va. 9—Chamberlain, R.
Conn. 5—Chamberlain Woodruff &
Scranton
Md. 28-30—Chapman, John J.
Pa. 88—Chapman, W. B.
Mass. 26, 77—Chase, F. J. & Co.
N.Y. 150-7—Chesebrough, Stearns
& Co.
Ill. 9-11—Childs & Co.
N.Y. 1056—Chubbuck, S. W.

Md. 182—Citizens Line
Va. 14—City of Petersburg
Md. 18—C., J. W. and Co.
Mo. 31—Claflin, Allen & Co.
Md. 32—Claridge, G. D. & Co.
R.I. 2—Clark and Anthony (Low 94)
N.Y. 30, 160—Clark James & Co.
N.Y. 159—Clark T. L.
Tenn. 8—Cleaves, C. C.
N.Y. 161—Clinton Lunch
N.Y. 753 Clinton's, Sir Henry,
House
Md. 34—Cloud House
Tenn. 1—Coal Creek Mining Co.
N.Y. 6—Cochran, J.   (Low 161)
Pa. 89—Cogan, Edward
N.Y. 9—Cogan, Edward
Mo. 5—Cohn, M. A.
Va. 2—Cole and Flinn
Md. 35—Cole, H. H.
Md. 37—Cole, James
N.Y. 163—Collins Ready Made Linen
N.Y. 164—Columbia Garden
Pa. 589—Co-Metallic Dollar of
Eutopia
Md. 39—Concordia
N.Y. 13—Coney Island Elephant
N.Y. 17—Coney Island Jockey Club
N.Y. 943, 1025—Congress Hall
(Hotel)
Ky. 2—Cook and Sloss
Mass. 27—Cook, Henry
N.Y. 166—Cooper Union
Pa. 103—Corporation of Philadel-
phia (Low 152)
Pa. 104—Covert, Wm.
Mo. 6—Cox, M. B. & Co.
Pa. 109—Cragin, I. L. & Co.
Ohio 6—Crew's Pyramidal Railway
Mass. 133—Crocker Bros. & Co.
Miss. 2—Croom & Hill - Hotel Dixie
N.Y. 167—Crossman, H. (Low 112)
N.Y. 16—Crown Steam Laundry
N.Y. 169—Crumble, W. D.
Mass. 30—Currier & Greeley
N.Y. 171—Curtis, John K.
N.Y. 19—Cutler, F.
Pa. 38—C.W.B. (Bender)
Mass. 35—Dadmun, F. W. & Co.
La. 4—Daquin Bros.

Mass. 34—Darby Dr., Consult
Conn. 25—Davenport
N.Y. 190—Day, Newell & Day
N.Y. 193—Dayton, J. H. (Low 114)
N.Y. 194—Dean
N.Y. 207—Delmonico
Pa. 114—Depuy, Thomas
N.Y. 208—Deveau, P. B. (Low 115)
Va. 3—Diamond Saloon
Pa. 122—Dickson White & Co.
Mich. 2—Dimmick, J.
Pa. 124—Disston, Henry
Pa. 125—Dobbins
Ohio 7—Dodd
Tenn. 17—Dodd
Ohio 8—Dodd & Co.
N.Y. 209—Dodge, J. Smith
Pa. 126—Doll, George & Co.
N.Y. 224-229 (471, 473, 477, 1033)—
    Doremus & Nixon
N.Y. 211-24 (394)—Doremus, Suy-
    dam & Nixon
Md. 44—Dorman, J.F.W.
Md. 42—Dorman's Stencil & Stamp
    Wks.
N.Y. 210—Dougherty, Philip A.
Pa. 127—Drown, Wm. A.
Pa. 129—Drown, W. A. & Co.
N.Y. 230—Druidical Exhibition
Ky. 7—Duncan Sanford
N.J. 4—Duseaman, T. (Low 148)
Mass. 36—Eastern R.R. Co.
N.Y. 165—Ebling's Columbian
    Garden
La. 8—Edgar, W. J.
Mo. 29—Edwill & Berry
N.Y. 231—Ehret, George
N.Y. 233—Eichler, John
Pa. 595—Eintracht monogram
Ga. 4—Eldorado Saloon
Ill. 42—Elgin National Watch Co.
Md. 46—Elliott, H. O. & Bro.
Mass. 36—ERR (Eastern RR Co.)
Ohio 11—Erwin, S. C.
Pa. 142—Evans & Watson
Md. 47—Evening News
N.Y. 232—Evening News
Ohio 12—Evens, P.
Ohio 15—Evens Sewing Machine
Md. 47—Falenstein G.

Tenn. 9—Fargason Sordes & Co.
N. Y. 234—Farmers & Mechanics
    Life Insurance Co.
Mass. 38—Farnsworth Phipps & Co.
Pa. 163—Feather, S.
N.Y. 238—Female Preventative
Mass. 39—Fero, George
N.Y. 240-1—Feuchtwanger, Dr. L.
N.Y. 242-6—Feuchtwanger 3 cents
    (Low 117-119)
N.Y. 247—Feuchtwanger Cent
    (Low 120)
Md. 51, 53—F.H.
Md. 54—FHF Co. (Federal Hill
    Ferry Co.)
N.Y. 248—Field, W.
Maine 3—Field, W. R.
N.Y. 249—Fifth Ward Museum
N.Y. 250—Finch Sanderson & Co.
R.I. 3—Finck, George
N.Y. 251—Fink's Hotel
Mo. 21—Fitzgibbons
N.Y. 263—Fitzgibbons Daguerreo-
    type Gallery
Pa. 164—Flanagan, R.
Pa. 166—Fleming, Dr. D. L.
La. 24—Folger & Blake
La. 9—Folger, Nathan C. (Low 121)
La. 10-20—Folger, N. C.
La. 21-22—Folger, N. C. & Sons
Mass. (21)—Folger, N. C. & Son
N.Y. (393)—Folger, N. C. & Son
Conn. 26—Forbes and Barlow
Md. 55—Fosdick Mitchell & Hild
Mich. 10—Foster and Parry
Ohio 14—Foster, J. Jr.
Mich. 12—Foster Martin & Co.
Miss. 3—Fotterall, Benjm. F.
N.Y. 265—Francis Patent Screws
Tenn. 11, 56—Francisco & Co.
Ill. 17—Francisco & Whitman
Tenn. 53—Francisco & Whitman
Tenn. 20—Francisco & Wiggin
Cal. 4—Frank, W. and Co.
N.Y. 266—Franklin & Co.
Ky. 42—Frazer, R. L.
N.Y. 268—Frederick's Pharmacy
N.Y. 275—French's Hotel
N.Y. 65—Friend & Black
Pa. 167—Fries Malseed & Hawkins

Pa. 162—F S (Low 149)
N.Y. 276—Furlong, E. P.
Pa. 171—Fussell, Henry B.
Md. 56—G & Co.
La. 25—Gaines, Charles C.
La. 27—Gasquet Parish & Co.
Md. 57—Geckie, Chas. W.
Pa. 172—Gercke, J. H.
Md. 61—Germania Maennerchor
Md. 184—Gibson (S.H.) & Son
        Gibbs, D. J.
N.J. 5—Gibbs, J. (Low 150)
N.Y. 277—Gibbs J.
N.J. 6—Gibbs W. (Low 151)
N.Y. 278—Gibbs W.
N.C. 1—Gilbert, D. J. Harnett
Ga. 1—Gilbert, J.
Pa. 178—Gilbert J. W.
N.Y. 279—Giroud, Inventor
N.Y. 280—Globe Fire Insurance Co.
Pa. 179—Goodyear & Sons
Pa. 181—Gordon, W.J.M.
N.Y. 286—Gosling's Restaurant
Md. 63—Gosman & Co.
N.Y. 267—Gould, D. H.
La. 28—Gowans, D. & Co.
Md. 64—Grannis & Taylor
Ohio 16—Gray's Bankrupt Store
Pa. 182—Great Union Pacific Tea
        Company
N.Y. 288—Green and Wetmore
Maine 4—Greenwood & Co.
Md. 47—Greenwood Park
N.Y. 291—Grimshaw, W. D.
N.J. 31—Guarantee Development Co.
Vt. 1—Gustin & Blake (Low 176)
Md. 65—Guth Chocolate Co.
Md. 66—Gutman Joel & Company
Tenn. 26—Haller & Ellis
N.Y. 292—Hallock & Bates
N.Y. 294—Hallock Dolson & Bates
Md. 67—Hamill, Chas. W. & Co.
Ill. 12—Hamilton & White
R.I. 4—Handy, W. A. (Low 78)
Ill. 13—Hannah & Hogg
N.Y. 676—Hannibal, The, of
        America
N.Y. 295—Hardie, A. W.
Md. 68—Hardy, Col.

Pa. 187—Harrbach's Original Wai-
        nut Candy
Pa. 190—Harrbach's Christmas
        Tree Ornaments
Pa. 191—Harmstead, James
Tenn. 58—Harris and Pearl
Tenn. 27—Harris A. O. & Co.
Pa. 190—Harris T. B.
N.Y. 300—Hart and Co.
Pa. 195—Hart and Co.
N.Y. 296—Hart Samuel and Co.
Pa. 198—Hart's Tea Store
Pa. 201 -Harvey, Samuel & Joseph
N.Y. 301—Haskins and Wilkins
N.Y. 10, 47—Haskins W. P.
        (Low 80)
R.I. 5—Hathaway, Ephraim A.
        (Low 74)
Ga. 7—Hausman, W. H.
N.Y. 302—Havens
S.C. 3—Haviland Stevens & Co.
Conn. 30—Hayden, I.
Conn. 4—Hayward, N.
Ga. 5—Haywood's Saloon
Mass. 31—Heidsick & Fils
N.Y. 1017—Henderson & Lossing
La. 30—Henderson & Gaines
La. 32—Henderson Walton & Co.
N.Y.42—Herr Alexander
Md. 69—Herring, H. (Low 173)
Mass. 4, 44—Hess and Speidel
Va. 11—Hess and Speidel
N.Y. 303—Hewett, Dr. J. A.
Ind. 1—Hildebrand & Co.
N.Y. 455—Hill, E.
N.Y. 305—Hill, L.
Ky. 14—Hirschbuhl, J. J.
N.Y. 341—Hoag, T.
Md. 70—Hochschild, Kohn & Co.
Ill. 14—Holden C N & Co.
Conn. 31—Holmes, Booth & Hayden
N.Y. 347—Hooks, Benjamin
Pa. 204—Hooper, Martin & Smith
N.Y. 351—Hoops, H. W.
Wis. 2—Hopkins, I. A.
Md. 71—Horn, H. J. & Co.
N.Y. 356—Horter, Charles D.
Conn. 5—Hotchkiss Hall & Platt's
Md. 72—Houck's Panacea
N.Y. 359—Houghton Merrill & Co.

Ky. 15—Howe Machine Co.
N.J. 7—Howell Works Garden
(Low 81)
Mo. 7—Huckel Burrows & Jennings
(Low 177)
N.Y. 360—Hudnut's Mineral
Pa. 206—Hugh's House
Mo. 33—Hume & Co.
Ala. 1—Hunt Pynchon & Jackson
Mass. 136—Huntley, A.
N.Y. 361—Huyler's
Cal. 3—Hyman, N. J.
Pa. 210-30—Idler, W.
N.Y. 368—Irving, L. G.
Pa. 231—Irvins, E.
Mo. 8—Jaccard, E. & Co.
Ky. 3—Jackson, C. N.
Mass. 24; Pa. 234—Jackson C. W.
La. 33—Jacob E.—Daguerreotype
Mass. 45—Jameson & Valentine
N.Y. 370—Jarvis, George A.
(Low 122)
N.Y. 405—J E
N.Y. 372—Jefferson Insurance Co.
Ill. 18—Jenchi, F. A.
N.Y. 373—Jenkins, William R.
N.Y. 378—Jennings, Wheeler & Co.
Miss. 1—Jewell, J. D.
Ill. 21—J H H
Ky. 19—J J F — St. Charles
Ky. 41—Johnson & Bros.
Pa. 3—Johnson Nimrod & Co.
N.Y. 396-402—Johnson Prof.
Pa. 238—Jones Exchange Hotel
N.Y. 403—Jones William G.
Cal. 6—Joseph B.
N.Y. 407—J P
N.Y. 1026—Judson, Hiram
Md. 76—Jury, Benjamin
Md. 18—J.W.C. & Co.
Md. 77—Kann's Busy Corner
N.Y. 409—Kayser, H & M & Co.
Md. 78—Keach
Cal. 7—Kelley, Wm.
Pa. 240—Kelly's Furniture
Ohio 17—Kemmeter, Geo. & Co.
Mass. 46—Kendall's
N.J. 32—Kennedy, S.
Md. 79—Kenny, C. D. Co.
Md. 80—Kensett

Md. 81—Kepler's
N.Y. (329) (445) (990)—Key
large letters
Pa. 265-285—Key and Co.
Pa. 258-263—Key F. C. & Sons
N.Y. (987)—Key F. C. & Sons
N.Y. (442)—Key F. C. & Sons
Pa. 364—Key, Wm. H. & Diehl
Pa. 249—Kilbride, G.
N.Y. 1064—Kingsley, T. L.
Ohio 19—Kinsey, E & D
N.Y. 411—Kipp, Brown & Co.
Tenn. 59—Kirkham, H & I
Ky. 20—Kirtland, F. S.
Wis. 7—Kleinsteuber, Chris.
Pa. 286—Kline, John W.
N.Y. 11—Knapp
N.Y. 412—Knapp J. C. Mfg. Co.
Md. 83—Knight, A.
Md. 84—Knight's Mineral Saloon
Pa. 290—Knoeppel, Frederick
Iowa 1—Kohn, A & Co.
Tenn. 28—Kohn Daron & Co.
Md. 60—Kola Pepsin
Pa. 518—Kossuth's, Thomas J.
N.Y. 413—Kruger, Th.
Md. 86—Kunkel's Opera Troupe
Md. 4—LA (Ansbeck)
N.Y. 21—Laborers' Union
N.Y. 414—Ladies Restaurant
Pa. 290—Lambert, A.
Ohio 20—Lamphears
N.Y. 416—Lane, David H.
N.Y. 417—Law, H.
Mass. 47—Learned & Co.
N.Y. 12—Leask
N.Y. 418—Leask, M.
N.Y. 419—Lehr, F.
N.Y. 420—Leighton, C.
N.Y. 581—Leopold del Meyer's
Concert
Md. 32—LePere and Richard
N.Y. 425—Leverett & Thomas
N.Y. 993—Levick
N.Y. 969—Levick, J.M.T.
N.Y. 426-63—Levick, J.N.T.
N.Y. 464—Liebertz, P.
Pa. 296-326—Lingg & Bro.
N.Y. 465-78—Loder & Co.
N.Y. 20—Loewe, J. C.

Mo. 12—Long, E.
Mo. 17—Long, H. H.
Pa. 327—Long, Wm. W.
Ohio 36—Loomis, A.   (Low 158)
N.Y. 479—Lorillard, P & Co.
N.Y. 485—Lovett
N.Y. 486—Lovett, Geo. H.
N.Y. 496—Lovett, J. D.
N.Y. 504—Lovett, R.
Pa. 330-56—Lovett, R. Jr.
Mass. 48—Low, John H. & Co.
Ky. 22—Luria, M. H.
N.Y. 507-18—Lyon, E.
La. 38—Lyons, L. W. & Co.
N.Y. 512—Macy, R. H. & Co.
Mass. 49—Mahoney's Clothing
N.Y. 515—Malcolm and Gaul
N.Y. 514—Mall Morsonic Amulet
Pa. 357—Malseed and Hawkins
N.Y. 518—Manhattan Watch Co.
Mo. 20—Manville, S.
N.H. 3—March Nath'l.   (Low 124)
Va. 15—Marks and Co.
N.Y. 521—Marshall & Townsend
N.Y. 1007-16—Marshall's, M. L.
Mass. 51—Marston, E. & Co.
Mass. 50—Marston R. & Co.
Md. 87—Marwell, W. G.
Pa. 363—Mason & Co.
Md. 88—Mason Baker (English?)
N.Y. 523—Matthews, John
Cal. 8—Maudit Circle de SF
Mass. 52—Maverick Coach
          (Low 116)
N.Y. 528—Maycock, S & Co.
          (Low 125)
Ohio 21—McClure, E. A.
N.Y. 8—McCormick's Park Skate
          Check
Md. 188—McGill and Moore
Maine 2—McKenny, Gunsmith
N.Y. 530—Meade Bros.
Mass. 53—Mechanical Bakery
Md. 89—Mechanics Hall
Mass. 54—Mechanics Saving Bank
Tenn. 31—Memphis Jockey Club
Tenn. 29—Megibben & Bro.
N.Y. 531, 534—Merchants Exchange
          (Low 96)
La. 41—Merle, John A. & Co.

R.I. 19—Merriam
Mass. 35, 78—Merriam, Joseph H.
Tenn. 30—Merrill, J. M. & Co.
N.Y. 536—Merritt & Langley
N.Y. 535—Merritt, J. G.
N.Y. 558—Meschutt's Metropolitan
          Coffee Room
Mass. 70—Messer, W. W.
N.Y. 563—Metropolitan Cave
N.Y. 572—Metropolitan Insurance
          Co.
N.Y. 581—Meyer, Dr. Leopold
Ky. 24—Miller, H. & Co.
Tenn. 32—Miller, M. H.
N.Y. 582—Miller's Hair Invigorator
Mass. 75—Milikins Hotel
Mass. 72—Milton, W. H.
Mass. 73—Milton, Wm. H. & Co.
Md. 90—Mitchell, J., People's Line
Ala. 2—Mobile Jockey Club
N.Y. 583—Model Artist Exhibition
N.Y. 585—Moffet, James, G.
Md. 91—Momenthy, B.
Md. 93—Monroe Association
Md. 94—Montebello Club
Md. 95—Moore and Brady
Mass. 126—Moore Bros.
Pa. 367—Morgan & Orr
Va. 33—Morgenstern, O.
Ga. 3—Morrison, J. & D.
Pa. 590—Morse's Literary Depot
N.Y. 838—Moses, M. H. & Co.
N.Y. 587—Moss' Hotel
N.Y. 614—Mott, Wm. H.
N.Y. 610—Motts
Pa. 4—Mt. Holly Paper Co.
Md. 97—Mount Vernon Club
N.Y. 616—Mullen, Wm. J.
Pa. 370—Mulligan, H.
Ohio 2, 21—Murdock & Spencer
Ohio 22—Murdock James
Pa. 374—Murphy, D. M.
N.Y. 617—Myers, Jim
Md. 98—National Brewing Co.
N.Y. 618—National Jockey Club
Pa. 378—Needles, P. H.
Tenn. 35—Nevils & Rose
N.Y. 500—New Congress Hall
Mass. 76—New England Dining
          Saloon

Pa. 2—Newman's Clothing Store
N.Y. 277—New York-Belleville USM
    Stage
Md. 101—New York Clothing House
Ala. 29—New York Crystal Palace
N.Y. 292, 948—New York Crystal
    Palace
N.Y. 619—New York Harlem Rail-
    road
N.Y. 534—New York Joint Stock
    Exchange
N.Y. 624—New York, S. D. & Co.
Mo. 21, 23—Nicholson's Grocery
Md. 99—Nonpareil
Mass. 79—Newlin & McElwain
Md. 102—N, W & Sons
    (Wm. Neumsen)
Md. 103—O'Brien's
N.Y. 1019—Olcott & Brothers
N.Y. 1018—Olcott Brothers
N.Y. 380—Omnibus Line
N.Y. 625—One Hundred Street
Md. 106—O'Neill & Co.
Pa. 594—Oppenheim, Simon
N.Y. 627—Parisian Varieties
N.Y. 626—Parmele, Edwin
N.Y. 628—Parmelee Webster & Co.
Ind. 2—Parry Mfg. Co.
Pa. 382—Partridge & Richardson
Md. 107—Patapsco Fruit Butter Co.
N.Y. 22—Patterson Bros.
Tenn. 36—Paul & Crockett
La. 44—PB   (Puech Bein Co.)
Ill. 22—Peacock, C. D.
Pa. 392—Peaelzer Bros.
N.Y. 632—Peale's Museum, etc.
Ill. 25—Pearson & Dana
Mo. 26—Pease, S. & Co.
N.Y. 368—Pease P. S. & Co.
Mass. 80—Peck and Burnham
N.Y. 1049—Peck, J. & C.
N.Y. 383—Pennsylvania Mutual Life
    Ins. Co.
Pa. 390—Pennypacker & Sibley
Pa. 1051—Percy E L.
Mass. 83—Perkins & Co.
Mass. 82—Perkins, E.
Md. 118—Peters, W.
Va. 14—Petersburg, City of
N.Y. 635—Phalon   (Low 127)

N.Y. 635—Phelan, Geo. E.
Pa. 103—Philadelphia Corporation
    of (Low 152)
Pa. 394—Philadelphia Museum
Pa. 400—Pickard, A.
Pa. 399—Pic-Nick & Sommernachts-
    fest
Va. 4—Piedmont Club
Va. 1—Piepenbring, E.
N.Y. 640—Pimmel, W.
N.J. 33—Pine, G.
Mass. 32—Piper and Co.
La. 42—Pitkin, Robert
Va. 36—Pizzini
Ill. 3—Plane & Jennison
Ill. 1—Plane, John & Co.
R.I. 19—Plastridge, A. A.
Md. 119, 121—Platt & Co.
Conn. 1—Platt, O. S.
Cal. 1—Pollemus
Mass. 84—Porter, Horace
R.I. 1—Porter, S.
Pa. 381—P P P
Ky. 29—Preissler, H.
N.Y. 644—Prentice, F.
N.Y. 645—Prescott's
Ky. 27—Preuser & Wellenvoss
Md. 123—Price Bros. & Co.
Md. 122—Price Bros.
Md. 124—Pringsheim
N.Y. 291—Prosse, Thos. & Son
R.I. 21—Providence Institute for
    Savings
Mo. 27—Prouhet, H.
N.Y. 646—Prudens
La. 43—Puech Bein & Co. (Low 82)
Iowa 2—Putzu's Clothing
Md. 125—Pyfer & Co.
Maine 7—Quebe, F.
Ky. 30—Quest, J. W.
N.Y. 765—Raffle
N.Y. 651—Rahm, Louis
N.Y. 38—Rahming, Edwin
Va. 5—Raine, Charles J.
Md. 127—Randall, F. O.
Del. 1—Randel, J. L.
N.Y. 654—Rathbone & Fitch
N.Y. 655—Redfield & Rice
Pa. 404—Rech, Jacob
Pa. 405—Reed, J.

Md. 129—Reid, P. J.
N.Y. 23—Reilly's Bazaar
Mass. 85—Reuter & Alley
Pa. 411—Rice, M. H.
Mass. 1—Richards, H M & E I
    (Low 83)
N.Y. 656—Richardson, Stephen
Pa. 416—Richardson, W & C
Pa. 417, 422—Richardson, W. H.
Fa. 421—Richardson, Wm. H.
N.Y. 657—Richardson, Wm. H.
Pa. 428—Rickett's Circus
Ohio 41—Rickey's Book Store
N.Y. 659—Riker, Abraham
    (Low 153)
N.Y. 661—Riker, J.L.
Md. 185—Ringgold, Reinhart
N.Y. 663—Risley & McCullum's
    Hippodrome
N.Y. 40—Rivinius
N.Y. 666-725—Robbins Royce &
    Hand
Conn. 6—Robinson, Alfred S.
N.Y. 729—Robinson Jones & Co.
    (Low 75)
N.Y. 27—Robinson, L.
N.Y. 726—Robinson R & W
    (Low 103)
N.H. 2—Roby, N. W.
Mass. 97—Rogers, J.S. & Bro.
Conn. 12—Rogers Smith & Co.
N.Y. 7—Roller Skating Association
N.Y. 731—Root and Co.
Pa. 433—Root M. A.
Ohio 23—Ross, Albert
N.Y. 735—Rowell, Geo. P. & Co.
Mass. 87—Roxbury Coaches
    (Low 129)
N.Y. 742—Royal Preventive
N.Y. 745—Ruggles, R. B.
Md. 130—Rullmann, W.
N.Y. 747—Russell, R. E. (Low 128)
Md. 131—Ruth, Francis J.
Mass. 88—Rutter, William
N.Y. 748—Sachem Oyster House
N.Y. 149-68—Sager, A. B. & Co.
N.Y. 770—Sampson, H. G.
Mass. 89—Sampson, .Z S.
Mo. 28—Sanders, C. G.
N.Y. 769—Sans Souci

Va. 38—Sauer, C.
Pa. 438—Sausse Dangler & Co.
Md. 132—Sauter, Frank
Va. 42—Schaefer Christ
Mass. 3—Schenck, S. B. (Low 84)
Mass. 1, 81—Schenck's Patent Plan-
    ing Mach.
N.Y. 779—Schmidt, Edward
Pa. 443—Schmidt, John K.
Md. 133—Schofield, Henry
N.Y. 782—Schoonmaker, W. N.
Pa. 1—Schroeder, Rudolph
Md. 134, 141, 145—Schutzen Park
Ill. 28—Schuttler, Peter
Md. 179—Schuetzen Park. W. Balto.
Mo. 34—Scott & Bros.
Pa. 449—Scott C. B. & Co.
N.Y. 786—Scott J. W. & Co.
Conn. 33-35—Scovill, J.M.L. & W.H.
    (Low 130)
N.Y. 802—Scovill Manufacturing Co.
N.Y. 805—Scovills Daguerreotype
    materials
Pa. 593—Scranton Stove Works
N.Y. 806—Sea Island Shirts
N.J. 9—Seaman, T. D. (Low 155)
N.Y. 39—Sears, B. & Co.
    (W. M. & B)
N.Y. 1067—Sedgwick
Md. 158—See Dem. T. Union
S.C. 14—Seegers, J. C. & Co.
Md. 148—Seger, Jacob
N.Y. 807—Seitz Bros.
N.Y. 469—Selleck Dr.
Pa. 456—Server, John H.
Md. 153—Shakespeare Club
Pa. 462—Shamcar & Hard
N.Y. 34—Sharpe, A. D.
Pa. 468—Sharpless, B.
Maine 5—Shattuck's, Dr., Water
    Cure
Ill. 27—Shaw, J. B.
Tenn. 37—Sheerer, J. W. & Co.
N.J. 23—Shridee, Alfred — Shreve
Md. 189—Shriver, (B.F.) & Co.
Md. 135—Shriver John L.
N.H. 3—Simes, William & Co.
    (Low 124)
Pa. 594—Simon Oppenheim
Tenn. 61—Singleton, R. H.

N.Y. 753—Sir Henry Clinton's House
N.H. 4—Sise, E. F. & Co. (Low 132)
N.J. 32—Slater, Walton & Co.
Pa. 475—Sleeper & Fenner
Tenn. 42—S. McD. & Co.
Pa. 479—Smith & Brother
Mo. 42—Smith & Ruger
N.Y. 821—Smith & Seward
Md. 156—Smith & Wicks
N.H. 1—Smith A. C.
N.Y. 1068—Smith C.A.M.
N.Y. 813—Smith Jas. S. & Co.
N.Y. 817—Smith F.B. & Hartman
Pa. 480—Smith James R.
Wis. 9—Smith J. McD.
Pa. 482—Smith Murphy Co.
Pa. 481—Smith Murphy & Co.
R.I. 6—Smith S.
Conn. 2—Smith Thadeus Ag't.
N.Y. 808—Smith's Clock Establishment (Low 133)
N.Y. 606, 823, 863, 909—Smithsonian House
Pa. 483—Snyder & Shankland
Md. 159—Soulsby, Robert
Tenn. 43—Southworth & Knight
Md. 191—Sovereigns of Industry
Md. 160—Spencer, L. C. & Co.
Ohio 29—Spencer, Wm. W.
Pa. 486—Spering, Good & Co.
Pa. 488—Spering, Mixsell & Inness
N.Y. 827—Squire & Merritt
N.Y. 832—Squire, Lewis L. & Sons
Ohio 3—Stanton, John
Mass. 90—Stanwood, H.B. & Co.
N.Y. 1052—Starbuck & Son (Low 156)
N.Y. 1022—Starr, Frederick
Mo. 30—State Savings Ass.
Pa. 489—Steel, Robert
Md. 162—Steinbach, Geo. P.
N.Y. 24—Stephenson's Jewelry Store
Pa. 490—Stevens, A. M.
Md. 164—Stevens, Chris
Pa. 591—Stevenson, W.
Ala. 27—Stickney & Wilson
N.Y. 839—Stiner, Jos. & Co.
N.Y. 838—Stiner Tea Company

Pa. 491—Stitz, John & Sons
Mo. 29—St. Louis Post Office
Pa. 500—Stokes Co.
Pa. 498—Stokes Granville
Pa. 501—Stolz's Segar Store
Pa. 502—Stoughton, Dr.
Mass. 135—Strange, E. W.
N.Y. 841-7—Strassburger & Nuhn
Md. 165—Strouse & Brothers
Ill. 40—Stumps, Peter
Ky. 36—Suit, S. T.
Pa. 503—Suive Eckstein & Co.
N.Y. 848—Suydam & Boyd
N.Y. 850—Sweeny, D. & Son
N.Y. 604, 850, 907—Sweeny's Hotel
N.Y. 865—Sweet, Ezra B. (Low 140)
N.Y. 867—Swift & Fargo American Hotel
Mo. 36—Swope, J. W.
Ala. 29—Sylvester & Co.
Md. 168—Tafelrunde Deutscher Maenne
N.Y. 877—Talbot, Allum & Lee
Tenn. 44—Tarbox N.Y. & Co.
La. 45—Tatout Brothers
N.Y. 890—Taylor & Son
Ky. 2, 32—Taylor & Raymond
N.Y. 891—Taylor & Richards
Pa. 504—Taylor A. B.
Pa. 512—Taylor Apothecary
Ill. 43—Taylor H. H. (obv.)
N.Y. 889—Taylor, J.M.
Pa. 513—Taylor, N.G. & Co. (See also Civil War tokens)
Tenn. 45—T. C. & Co.
Md. 166—Teutonia Club
N.Y. 892—Theatre, The - at New York
La. 46—Theodore
N.Y. 894—Third Avenue Railroad
Ohio 31—Thomas & Robinson
Ky. 33—Thomas, H. E. & Co.
Pa. 518—Thomas, J. Kossuth's Ex.
N.Y. 898—Thomas, R. F.
N.Y. 608-865-899—Thompson, A.D.
N.Y. 411—Thompson, S. H.
N.Y. 25—Thomson, W. A.
Pa. 51—Thornton, James
Cal. 9—Thurman & Zinn
Mass. 129—Tilly Haynes & Co.
Md. 167—Toland, William

N.Y. 913—T. P. D.
N.Y. 915—Traphagen Hunter & Co.
Md. 170—Trausch, Chas.
N.Y. 920—Tredwell, Kissam & Co.
N.Y. 919—Tredwell, S. L.
N.Y. 922-5—Trested, Richard
Md. 172—Turner, Robert & Son
Mass. 91—Tuttle, C. F.
Md. 173—Twaits, T. D. & Co.
Mich. 4—Tyler, C. C. & Co.
N.Y. 926—Tyson & Co.
Md. 177—UBV monogram (Ukel
    Braesig Verein)
Md. 174—U. S. Mfg. Co.
N.Y. 928—Upson's Capital
Pa. 524—Vallee, John E.
Wis. 10—Van Cott, A. B.
N.Y. 932—Vanderbilt Isaac Stevens
Mo. 37—Vandeventer, J. W. & Co.
Mo. 38—Vandeventer, J. W.
N.Y. 933—Van Nostrand & Dwight
Ohio 32—Variwig, H.
N.Y. 934—Venten's D. Needle
    Threaders
Mass. 93—Vinton, C. A.
Mo. 35—W. & H. V.
La. 48—Waler, J. Hall & Walton
    (Low 85)
N.Y. 35—Walsh's General Store
    (Low 99)
La. 50—Walton & Co.
La. 49—Walton, Walker & Co.
    (Low 106)
Pa. 532—Wanamaker & Brown
N.Y. 935—Ware, James T.
Va. 44—Waring, W. L.
N.Y. 936—Warner
Pa. 533—Warner, Charles K.
N.J. Warrick & Stanger
Conn. 36—Waterbury Brass Co.
Conn. 27—Waterbury House
N.Y. 941—Waters, Horace & Sons
Pa. 530—Watson, James
Pa. 570—Weidner, A. J.
Ohio 33—Weighell & Sons
Cal. 12—Weil & Levi
Md. 178—Weil Moritz H.
N.Y. 945—Welch, Uriah
N.Y. 946—Wellenamp, Hugo
Md. 179—W. Baltimore Schutzen
    Park

Tenn. 46—Western Foundry
N.Y. 948—West's H.B. Trained Dogs
Tenn. 52—W. H. & Co.
Ky. 34—Whaley, Sherman P.
Mass. 94—White Bros. & Co.
Pa. 574—White W. H. & Co.
Pa. 575—Whitman & Son
N.J. 18—Whitney Glass Works
N.J. 16—Whitney S.A.
S.C. 5—Wilbur, W. W.
Mass. 98—Wilkins, S. L. (Low 86)
Mass. 95—Willard, Alfred
Pa. 579—Williams Dr.
Pa. 580—Williams F.G. & Co.
N.Y. 953—Williams Rd. Union Hall
N.Y. 18—Williamsburg Brewing Co.
N.Y. 954—Willis & Brothers
Ill. 41—Willoughby Hall & Co.
Tenn. 48—Wilson Laird & Co.
Pa. 584—Wine Store
N.Y. 955—Wise, A.
Tenn. 47—Wiswall, J. M. & Co.
Md. 102—W. N. & Sons
    (Wm. Neumsen)
Tenn. 50—Wolf, M.
N.Y. 958—Wolfe Clark & Spies
N.Y. 957—Wolfe C & D
Ky. 35—Wolfe George
N.Y. 956—Wolfe's Schiedam
    Schnapps
Va. 18—Wolff, James E.
Ohio 34—Wood & Harrison
Md. 180—Woodale, Wm. E.
N.Y. 966—Woodcock, Wm. P.
N.Y. (333), (448)—Woodgate & Co.
N.Y. 969-999—Woodgate & Co.
N.Y. 964—Wood's Minstrels
Pa. 585—Wood's Museum
N.Y. 1000—Wright & Bale
Mass. 96—Wright, S. & Co.
N.Y. 1004—Wyman
N.Y. 1006—Y & Co.
La. 51—Yale C., Jr. & Co.
N.Y. 1028—Yates, A. C.
Pa. 587—Yates, A. C. & Co.
Md. 181—Yinger, A. Ellicotts Mills
N.Y. 1005—Young & Wood
Ohio 35—Zanoni & Bacciocco
Md. 182—Z, B.F. & Co., Citizen's
    Line (Benj. F. Zimmerman)